Sometimes Shells Make Sand

Sometimes Shells Make Sand

A story of love, loss, ALS,
and an unruly Labradoodle

JULIE DOYLE CULLEN

Wyatt-MacKenzie Publishing
DEADWOOD, OREGON

Sometimes Shells Make Sand

A story of love, loss, ALS, and an unruly Labradoodle

Julie Doyle Cullen

ISBN: 978-1-954332-18-8
Library of Congress Control Number: 2021946784

Wyatt-MacKenzie Publishing
DEADWOOD, OREGON

www.WyattMacKenzie.com

Dedication

For my mom, Suzanne Marie Doyle,
who loved nothing more than a good story,
a silly laugh, and a life filled with her special people.
My heart still aches, I miss you dearly and
look forward to seeing you again Mom.

Table of Contents

Prologue

I HAVE HAD A CHANCE to calm down and slow the spasmodic gasps between my sobs. I am taking deep breaths while a few stray tears trickle down my cheeks. Time has roamed, and I'm not sure how long I have been sitting on the cool tile of our first-floor half bath, but it seems like an eternity. I have a feeling of temporary safety and a sense of calm in this small space. The room was painted a pale yellow two years ago, and I think the serene tint is helping ease my mind. I am trying to decide if I will ever leave this room when I catch a glimpse of the skin above my kneecaps. What the hell is happening to my body? It seems like no one ever talks about how the knees begin to wrinkle, but they really should. Mine are looking quite furrowed at this angle, and I really need to invest in a powerful moisturizer.

Obviously, I'm easily distracted these days, and this knee obsession proves my point. Perhaps it's a coping mechanism. I'm not sure. In fact, I'm not sure of much anymore. To be completely honest, I am caught up in life's shitstorm and I'm not sure I can handle it.

Winnie, Mom's charcoal-colored Labradoodle, is sniffing and whining just outside the door. I can see her dark wet nose shoved against the opening under the floor. That's when I realized that I can't hide forever. I've got to face everything head-on. This breakdown will have to wait for another time. Right now, I need to refocus and regroup.

Then I hear a voice crackle over the monitor: "Jules, can you come here?"

"Just a second, I'm coming," I blurt out a little too quickly, like I have something to hide. Then I realize that I don't even sound like myself.

I quickly wipe my face as I open the door and startle Winnie to her feet. "Sorry, girl. Let's get back in there. She needs us."

Chapter 1
The Paper

I OPENED THE HEAVY GLASS doors to the hallway that led to the executive offices. The air was different in this part of the newspaper building; it smelled like privilege and rich hazelnut coffee. Not at all like a newsroom with desks piled high with papers and people shouting at each other. Or the advertising sales department, where my office door was always open and there was usually a line three-people deep to complain or ask advice about a disgruntled client. Doors were always closed in the executive suites, and secretaries looked quietly busy at their organized desks as they guarded the executives' doors. I rounded the corner of the hallway and stopped to check in with Mallory, assistant to Josh Canton, the publisher.

"Hi, Mallory, how are you? I wondered if you'd made it back from your vacation; I haven't seen you in a week." I always talked a little softer in this part of the building because my normal loud voice felt out of place.

"Hey, Julie. Yes, it was a family vacation and honestly, I'm glad to be back at work to get some peace. The kids fought about every-thing and complained if they weren't constantly on social media. I'm pretty much failing as a mom and when I'm here, I don't have to think about that—which is great."

"Yup, good times. Well, we're glad you're back here to relax." We both laughed, and she lightly knocked on Josh's door and let me in.

This was not a pre-planned meeting; I was summoned spur of the moment, which happened sometimes. It has been happening more often lately since we started this chaotic merger.

Josh was sitting behind his desk with his back to me, working on his laptop. His office was large and had a good amount of masculine energy with dark grass-cloth wallpaper and leather chairs. I sat in my usual spot at the long conference table.

"Hi Josh, how are you doing?" He stopped and walked over to join me at the conference table but said nothing. The lack of response jabbed me a bit since this was very unlike our usual light exchanges.

"Julie, you know how I feel about you. I have tried to guide your career whenever I could, and right now I am damn concerned about your future. More than concerned, I am worried about you! The direction regarding the merger has been clear and yet, on many occasions, you have questioned that direction," Josh said sternly as he adjusted his chair at the mahogany table.

My mind focused quickly on the topic at hand: we had been arguing about a few points of contention in the merger with our digital company. "Come on, Josh. You know as well as I do that these Alliance corporate assholes are making mistakes. I have been silent on many things, but some things I can't be quiet about. For one, we haven't even considered what our customers want, and this will backfire when it comes to our bottom line. Their priorities are all screwed up, and I know you see it, too!"

"At this point, it's out of our hands. Yes, I agree mistakes are being made, but this train is moving down the tracks and you need to get on board. We can't keep arguing with them over minor points; it's slowing down the process. If you can't get in line 100 percent, you will need to think about your options," he added sheepishly. He didn't seem comfortable getting tough with me.

"Well, I *do* have issues and I don't consider them minor points! The biggest problem for me is that they're just throwing revenue—and ultimately people—down the drain because they know they'll achieve their goals by reducing personnel costs. They will let most of these people go, and those folks don't deserve that. You and I know that's what it will come down to, and it makes me sick!" I had raised my voice without realizing it and he seemed taken aback. The executive wing was reserved for complicit whispers and everyone knew it. He made a note on a nearby legal pad and then looked at me with a blank expression. It made me think he had practiced this look in the mirror to make sure it gave nothing away.

After a long and uncomfortable pause, I said what I knew had been coming. Still, I was surprised to hear it aloud. "Leaving is the right thing for me. I can't agree with this process all in, or the fact that most of our dedicated employees are going to lose their jobs because of this bullshit merger. They see these people purely as expensive liabilities. If you want me to meet with this extended family—people I genuinely care about—and tell them they're out, I just won't do it."

We sat there in silence until Josh finally spoke in a very measured tone. "Please think about what you're saying. This is an important moment."

My face was hot, my mind jumbled. I felt like someone had picked me up and thrown me into a high-speed blender. My throat was suddenly very dry, and I was aware that I needed a drink of water but pushed that thought aside and sat, frozen.

After another uncomfortable pause, he added, "I was really dreading this, but I guess you just made your decision." Josh said this as he slid a large envelope toward me that had been hiding beneath his legal pad. He apparently already knew how this meeting was going to conclude. The thought that the paperwork had already been ready and waiting shook me hard. What was the plan if I'd stayed? Rip it up? Save it for the next crisis? I felt my stomach turn, and a small voice inside repeating *please don't let me vomit, don't you dare cry, don't give him any emotion.*

It didn't seem real, but the buyout agreement was right there in front of me. I scanned it quickly. The zeros and the commas jumped out at me and started to look like damaged salvation.

"Take your time, Julie. You don't have to sign it today. I'm sure you'll want your own attorney to check it out as well."

And then, surprisingly, there was a bit of relief. I had subconsciously known that a major power struggle was occurring within the company, I just didn't have it in me to join the fight anymore. Was this how I really wanted to cap my twenty years of sacrifice and hard work? Reading those words felt like a slow-motion detonation. I thought of myself as only a signature away from gone, but I wanted this to end. I was ready to go.

After processing the gravity of the moment and being keenly aware that Josh was still studying me, it flashed in my head like a thunderbolt. I needed to get out of this office! But the important thing was to remain calm under pressure. Instead of unleashing a long string of curse words and insults, I needed to stay professional.

"Yes. I will have my attorney look it over and follow up with any concerns."

"Good idea, Julie. Also, I have been thinking that it will be best if today is your last day since we know the team will be very shaken by your departure. We have so much going on with this merger that it would be better to keep the disruption to a minimum. Do we understand each other?"

It wasn't a question so much as a statement. My head pounded. There was so much I wanted to say, but I remained quiet as I pushed my chair and walked toward the door. Josh held out his hand and started going on about my great career and all we have accomplished, but I was only half-listening. I was more focused on getting out of the building so I could have a much-needed breakdown!

I got past Mallory with no problem since she was on the phone. She waved to me as she continued her conversation. I rounded the corner and was just to the double glass doors when the last person I wanted to see at that moment was heading straight toward me. Fuck-face Tiffany! The very definition of a fuck-face, someone who lulls you into a false sense of security and then screws you for their own benefit.

"Hi Julie, how are you?"

"Oh, really great, how about yourself?"

"Busy, but good. I was just called to Josh's office. Is something going on?"

"Oh yeah, there is definitely something going on. I'm sure you're about to hear all about it."

I had not stopped walking although she paused in the hallway like she wanted to have a longer conversation. I got by her and never looked back. I was happy I did not have a small pistol hidden in a garter belt or a shiv up my sleeve as I would have probably ended up in jail.

When I was first introduced to Tiffany, she was the director of operations for our digital counterpart out of New York. She was friendly enough, but what I didn't know then was that she had it out for me. As much as we try to be team players, women often succumb to this competitive wrestling match just as much as men. I didn't realize until it was too late that we were going to be engaged in a silent competition, locked in a battle for the top. She was tall, slightly overweight, and had a passion for outrageous style. Sometimes she would show up with bright pink streaks or shaved sides in her hair. This stood out like a sore thumb in our conservative business. It seemed acceptable because she was on the digital product side and from the New York office. We had a few pleasant lunches together where we munched on Cobb salads and talked about the client base and how to move more of the revenue over to digital products. I liked her at first and told her exactly what I thought when we discussed new business models that seemed too aggressive or overpriced for the market. She would take that information back to New York to paint me as uncooperative. First off, I had hoped for a sisterhood. She seemed to agree with me on many of the concerns and since there was good progress, I didn't think much of the conversations. Secondly, and much more importantly, what kind of name is "Tiffany" for someone involved in a gritty corporate battle? Tiffany is not the evil name of a scheming ball-buster. You just don't expect your nemesis to have a name that is synonymous with handcrafted glass lamps and high-end jewelry. I felt at ease with someone named Tiffany.

Some rumors also had me skeptical of her business skills. Supposedly, she'd had an affair with a former publisher of a smaller paper in the group. This publisher just happened to be the under-achieving nephew of our New York owners, and he was married. It was kept incredibly quiet while she mysteriously earned a few major promotions up to the corporate office. As with most rumors, they were unsubstantiated, but they circulated through manage-ment anyway. In hindsight, she didn't have the credentials or demeanor of someone who I should have been worried about on the surface. You just don't expect your sterling career and every-thing you worked for to come undone in a matter of months, but that is exactly what happened.

My suspicion came true when Josh named Tiffany the general manager of the entire operation after the merger. Immediately after I departed, I heard the announcement was made at a manda-tory department meeting. There were phone calls, emails, and texts of disbelief that I had left. I also heard there were gasps and tears at the meeting; most people knew this was the beginning of the end.

They methodically started letting people go with minimal sev-erance packages and nothing much else for the decades they had dedicated to the newspaper. Staff members from management positions all the way to clerical spots were called into a glass-walled conference room and given the standard five-minute speech and departure envelope for everyone to see. It was cold and calculated with no regard for the years of commitment each person had invested except for the difference in the dollar amounts. I was stunned and horrified as I heard about the process. It was a sad time and right at the holidays, which was additionally cruel. Corporate wanted all of this wrapped up before the new year began.

I'd breezed into my office to grab my purse, having avoided my assistant and anyone else who might try to get my attention along the way. I would come back at night or on the weekend to get my personal items, who cares? I somehow made it down to the parking level and found my car. I drove home on autopilot. The tears were streaming down as I cried openly. My heart ached for myself and all the people I cared about in that big, old building. I worried that my inability to stay and fight was cowardly. I thought about situations I should have handled differently. All these small snippets of scenarios where maybe I was too outspoken and should have held my tongue.

I came up in the ranks when women started as administrative assistants or in low-level clerical and sales positions without much influence. There were very few women in executive positions in the newspaper industry at that time unless they were family of the owners. In fact, in older buildings, the men's restrooms outnumbered the ladies' two to one. I worked extremely hard, including a lot of late nights, and pushed through many innovative ideas over the years. Sometimes, I felt like I knew the after-hours cleaning crew better than some of the members of my staff. And, if I am being honest, I'm sure that being a strawberry-blonde with long legs didn't hurt my career along the way. I was never technically sexually harassed, but I could often see the wheels turning in the man-brains when I walked into a conference room in a great dress. As women, we understood the challenges.

Once, I attended a video conference call with our attorney team in New York to discuss contract language for a large client. There was a big screen in our conference room and one in theirs as well. We could see them on our screen and vice versa. This was the latest technology at the time and quite intriguing. A small square in the upper right corner showed an image of what they were seeing from our room. I noticed that I was positioned directly in front and that my legs were clearly visible under the conference table. I had on a skirt and high heels and was admiring my legs on the screen. I have to say, I looked rather good. So, I started crossing my legs under the table to check out the image on the screen. It was a boring meeting. And then I looked up and noticed that all the male attorneys on the screen were very attentively watching me, too. As I said, it was a boring meeting for all of us. But at that moment, I knew no one was thinking about a client contract anymore. I got used to some of this attention, but I also learned the importance of being truly knowledgeable and competent in a meeting. It was imperative to understand the corporate environment and to always work hard. Now, it seemed that the years of trying to get and stay ahead must have finally caught up to me. Now I was ready to get out. There was no way to save the day in this sad situation.

How was I going to download all of this to Mark? Just as that thought revealed itself, I heard the garage door start its humming climb. He came in and tossed his keys on the counter.

"Jules, you're home? What's up?"

"Hi, yup, I'm home."

With one look at me, he knew something was very wrong. "Oh no, what happened?"

I did not hold back and began sobbing again as I blurted out fragments of the story. He held me to his chest and just listened until I came up for a breath of air.

"Oh no, Julie, what the hell? Did this all happen today? Wow, I'm so sorry, baby. Come over here and sit down." He pulled me to the family room sofa where I was able to relay a much more coherent version of the meeting. Talking to him calmed me down and we discussed our next steps.

There was some guilt because the generous buyout offered me a lot of options. I could take some time off while I looked for another job or start a business of my own. My next step wasn't clear, but I had the luxury of time to consider my options. I was almost fifty, I was recently remarried, and Mark was on board with whatever I wanted to tackle next. He was always in my corner, and that's the reason that I married him. Each of us had proclaimed after our divorces that we would never get married again. At that time, we were both very settled into our single lives, with grown children, homes, and retirement funds. We tried to maintain a long-distance relationship and enjoy some weekends and trips together. But as the months went by and we were spending all our available time together, we knew it was the right move to become an official couple and make the commitment. There were a few past marriages between us, so we kept it simple with a ceremony on the beach in St. Thomas. We took a two-week Caribbean vacation and knew we had something special.

He is smart, successful, and a wonderful partner. It is reassuring to know that there is someone in my corner when life takes a hard turn. Most of the time, I have only relied on myself. I am grateful we found each other.

My first marriage, to my college sweetheart, lasted seventeen mostly great years until we just grew apart. We quit wanting to spend time together. Our ideas and plans started to seem miles apart and our connection faded. Looking back, we silently let that destroy us. That's what happens when you get married too young and people change. But he is an amazing father to our daughter, Kylie, and that makes all the difference. I learned a lot from my first marriage. Mark had been married before as well, and we were both determined to make this relationship last.

After talking with our attorney, I finally signed and mailed the agreement back to Josh. I was sure that a change in my career would be a minor bump in the road.

Chapter 2
The Mall

AFTER THE BUYOUT, it felt weird to get up in the morning and not have a place to go. I had always fantasized about it, as many people do when they feel overworked. The luxury of having time on your hands makes you feel like you're getting away with something and that you will soon be in trouble. There were a few job offers right out of the gate, but they were similar to the one I had just left, and I was determined to do something different.

"Julie, you need to relax and enjoy this time. You've earned it," my mom said on numerous occasions.

"I can't say that I actually earned it, Mom. I refused to be a part of a bloody corporate takeover and took the easy way out by leaving quietly with a bag of money."

"Oh, come on. You're making this dramatic. You just don't have the poor judgment to go along with a flawed plan that's going to ruin the lives of people you love. You're a good person and you know that."

My mom had a way of turning your perceived shortcomings into admirable qualities that at the end of it are a tribute to her parenting. It was a gymnastic maneuver that many moms have mastered.

"While you're planning your next big move, why don't you take the opportunity to spend some time with your mom? For example, you like to exercise, so instead of that boring treadmill, why not walk with me in the mornings?"

Oh, God. The start of a sales pitch. She had been trying to get me to join her for morning mall walks, and this was the 900th time she'd asked me. Mall walking seemed like a way of giving up. It was mostly older folks who needed human interaction as they tried to prolong their lives by walking in a stuffy mall in nondescript jeans and sad excuses for tennis shoes. I was sure that I'd be the youngest person there at the age of forty-nine, and that was troubling.

"Do you remember when you and your sister ambushed me and told me I was a fat ass who's edging ever closer to a paralyzing stroke and needed to get some exercise?" she asked. "You had mentioned that you didn't look forward to diapering me in my post-stroke days."

I didn't remember it quite like that, but it was pointless to correct her.

"Oh, so now the guilt. I knew that would be next. And to clarify, you're much better off since starting this and have better legs and a tight ass, so ... you're welcome."

"Just come with me a few times, and if you don't like it you can go back to your boring upscale yoga health club with a juice bar and hot yoga classes for super-skinny housewives." She said this with a smirk, which I still picked up through the telephone.

"They're not really called 'yoga health clubs,' but whatever. All right, I'll give it a chance and walk with the mall zombies. Meet you there at, say, 8:00 in the morning?"

I hung up knowing my path was set on commercial carpet and mixed-tile floor in a one-mile track bordered by unobtainable-sized mannequin bodies and clearance sales.

The mall opened at exactly 8:00 a.m., and the stores opened at 10. Walkers started to gather early at three different doors to get let in by the security guard. My mom was a creature of habit and liked to park at the door by Saks for her morning access. She looked at me when I walked up like I was someone she didn't expect to see there. She must have thought that I would cancel.

She looked pointedly at her watch and said, "8:11. Thanks for being on time."

"OK, so I'm here. Let the humiliation begin," I said.

"You may need to work on that attitude, missy—zombies are kind of emotionless," she said, now smug and giggling.

We filed inside and hung our coats on a row of rental strollers. This must be the thing to do: it was covered with fleece pullovers, tacky embroidered sweatshirts, and down-filled vests.

The "walkers" were a mixed group and mainly fit into the following profiles: overweight men who had been told to exercise by their cardiologist, retired individuals mostly in small groups of three or four that could be further divided into men who talked about finances and politics, women who met at church or in a book club, and younger moms who walked on alternate days between Pilates classes. There were also a few random profiles: a young mom with an infant in tow trying to lose the post-pregnancy weight, and couples walking while holding hands after being referred there by their marriage counselor or a church "Strong Marriage" group. I must admit, these couples were the most unsettling to watch. It was like they were serving out a prison sentence. There were also folks who were trying to get some exercise or rehab after an accident. Mom fit into a group all her own: a walker making fun of these groups in hopes of meeting an eligible and age-appropriate man. I had the same hopes for her.

Her regular walking partner was her friend, Lorri, who was currently in Florida—Heaven's waiting room—for a few months. They met in a somewhat unorthodox way. Right after my divorce, I was dating a man from California who came to Michigan regularly for business. He was originally from here and had family living in our city. Lorri was his mother and in our three-year relationship, our moms became great friends. Their relationship survived and thrived while ours did not. I loved Lorri and was so happy that they were friends. My mom didn't have many friends because she was a lot to handle and got pissed off for the craziest reasons. She once stopped seeing a close work friend because she asked Mom to go camping. My mom saw camping as an activity of someone who couldn't be trusted. Why would anyone want to live outside in the dirt and pretend to be homeless?

There was one walking gang that seemed to interest her. It was a group of men that I named the "Mantastics." There were three or four of them depending on the day and while they walked the mall they talked about politics, investments, and current events. They were attractive, and you could tell they had been even more handsome in their prime. They were also still interested in females even while wearing ill-fitting sweatshirts and baggy jeans, and those sad athletic shoes. You could tell because they would size you up and say "hello" with a twinkle in their eyes as you passed. Often there was even a small wave or finger point. Mom claimed they were new to the walking scene, and there was quite a bit of interest from the ladies. It was oddly funny, like going to a mall of horny preteens but with hip problems and the occasional incontinence.

"Oh, this is great," Mom said. "I can use you as bait to meet these guys."

"OK, now this is getting good. I have time on my hands, and this sounds fun, so why not?" I said, amused. This mall-walking world had a dark underbelly that I had no idea existed, and I was intrigued.

So, we walked three days a week and it was kind of enjoyable, if for no other reason than to get some great one-on-one time with my mom, and the comic relief was a nice bonus. The following week, I picked her up at her house to walk, but there was a twist that day.

"Hi Julie, I didn't want to tell you in advance because I knew you would have snide comments, but the Mall Walking Club has their monthly breakfast this morning and we are going. This is a well-attended event and a great way to meet people."

"Oh wow, Mom, this sounds awful. And by people, you mean the Mantastics, right? This is a great way to meet them?"

"I couldn't care less about that group of old guys. I'm just interested in expanding my social circle," she commented quietly while grabbing a jacket. "Also, we better hurry since anything free is a drug for these folks. It'll be a mob scene."

I was trying to get to the door but having trouble fending off her crazed Labradoodle, Winnie. She had bad habits like grabbing your clothes with her teeth, jumping up on you, and the favorite: a stealth snout in the crotch while you were distracted by the first two moves. Mom loved this dog and had adopted her from a no-kill rescue shelter two years previously. When I found out about her determination to adopt a dog, I was somewhat concerned since my mom had suffered a string of what the family refers to as "the pet problems."

The history began when we got our first dog as kids. He came to our house from an elderly couple who could no longer care for him. His name was Schultz, and he was a dachshund. Immediately upon arriving, he took to hiding under the kitchen table. We couldn't lure him out with treats or any other incentives and if we tried to pull him out, he would nip at us. Finally, after a few months of misery and near misses of breaking skin, Schultz made a run for it, out an open patio door and back to the home of his original owners. They telephoned my mother to let her know he had arrived on their doorstep. We never saw Schultz again. Strike one.

As the years went by, my mom and dad decided it was time to get a puppy for our family. The thought was that the kids were old enough to help with dog care. They went to a breeder and came home with a nine-week-old Airedale terrier we named Winston Churchill. He was adorable and received a lot of attention from all of us. He was a great dog most of the time, but par for the course, at about three years old, he started to snap at people. My grandmother came for a visit and Winston bit her in the hand when she tried to pet him, and she needed four stitches. After much family discussion and tears, Winston Churchill went to the farm. Strike two.

Grief-stricken about the loss of Winston, my younger sister, Jenny, convinced my mom to let her get a rabbit that she named Clover. Clover resided in a large cage in the garage but was also allowed in the house and the backyard playing with my sister. Because of possible overfeeding, Clover became a huge rabbit and weighed more than eighteen pounds. One day, fat Clover got out of her cage in the garage and Mom came home and unknowingly ran her over with the car. It was a horrible scene that scarred us for years. Strike three.

With this tragic history, there was a valid reason to be concerned over my mother adopting a new pet. Before she got Winnie, Mom had once stopped a sweet young family walking along the boardwalk in the lakeside town of Grand Haven to ask them what kind of dog they had. They told her it was a Labradoodle and that it was a great family dog. This breed also fit my mom's favorite dog qualities: shaggy hair hanging in the eyes and adorable, floppy ears. That clinched it for Mom. She immediately started calling local shelters to see if they had any Labradoodles. Most of the receptionists were kind and told her that wasn't a common breed at shelters. They all explained that their dogs are usually mixed breeds that need rescuing, and not designer dogs. Some of them even downright laughed at her and let her know—with more than a hint of sarcasm—that if they ever did get one, she would be their first call. To her credit, that did not deter her; she put her name on the list of every shelter within an hour radius to get a Labradoodle. She was willing to wait it out.

A full year later, she received a call from Madison's Sanctuary. They had a Labradoodle! Winnie was abandoned as a puppy and wandered the streets for a while until she was picked up and brought to the no-kill shelter. Winnie had been there for a few months because she was wild and needed a lot of training before she could be adopted. There was a long list of people who wanted her but after several meet-and-greets, she always ruined her chance. There was entirely too much jumping, clothes biting, and general chaos. My mom felt a kinship with her and was intrigued by her crazy personality. Why a shelter would pair a seventy-plus-year-old woman who lived alone with a crazed young dog was beyond me, but that was the current situation.

It was during a casual phone call that I found out she finally got the dog.

"Julie, you'll never believe it, but I met my new best friend today and you have to come over to meet her. She is short, very hairy, drools a bit, and has terrible breath. I think you are going to love her."

"Mom, you're talking about a dog, right?"

"Yes, I just picked her up from the shelter. She is a black Labradoodle, about a year old. I know there'll be some challenges because she's scared of most noises, doesn't like to get in the car, and can't quite figure out stairs, but I'm sure we can get over all of that."

That was all before she knew about the clothes biting and other crazy shenanigans. My mother had a dog trainer "on retainer" who was going to make big bucks on this project. Hell, Winnie was even allowed on the furniture—not that you could keep the wild child off. As kids, *we* were barely allowed on the furniture. Together, the two found a groove of sleeping late, watching reality television, and sometimes, eating donuts for dinner.

The next day, after distracting Winnie by throwing her favorite ladybug toy, we loaded up and headed to the mall. The breakfast was held at Max & Erma's, a cute food court restaurant with the ingenious motto "every guest leaves with a smile." They had popular all-American low-calorie selections like the garbage burger. The breakfast buffet was a display of yogurt, various muffins, bagels, juice, and coffee. The restaurants in the mall had to host one of these breakfasts on a six-month rotation for the walking club, and it didn't look like they were out to impress with this effort. Despite the limited selection, the place was buzzing with activity. I got some coffee and yogurt and sat in a booth while my mom greeted people she knew. There was a lot of socializing, reminding me of a Greek mixer from college days. I could not believe that I was doing this; I needed to reexamine my life at this point!

Anyway, my mom finally landed in the booth, and soon, the Mantastics sent a handsome representative complete with a full head of salt-and-pepper hair to talk to us.

"Hi, ladies. How are you this morning? My name is Kent, and I noticed you walking together. We have a bet, and I'm going to say—mother and daughter? You're both beautiful and there is a resemblance, am I right?"

Nicely played, Kent. My mom was smiling. "Well, I should be upset that you think I could be the mother of this recently unemployed middle-aged lady, but you added 'beautiful,' so I'll let it slide. Yes, this is my daughter. My name is Suzanne, and this is Julie."

Typical. She threw me under the bus with the "unemployed middle-aged" comment, but I really didn't care. Technically and unfortunately, they were both on point.

Kent chuckled and I could see that they might be finding each other amusing. "I have been coming here with some of my old work pals from Ford. We walk about three days a week," he said.

"It's a great way to get some exercise, especially in the winter months," Mom said, trying to pretend she had not noticed the Mantastics before.

"Can I get you ladies any refills on your coffee?" Kent said, looking at our cups.

"No, but thanks so much. Trying to cut back on the caffeine," my mom added almost seductively.

The tone seemed to catch Kent slightly off guard. "Well, I'll be seeing you ladies around. Nice to meet you both." He turned to join his pals, who were heading out the door as they eyed up Kent's progress.

"Well, that was interesting. I'm sure that he only came over here to meet you," Mom said.

"Now why in the hell do you say things like that, Mom? He was focused on you the whole time."

"The reason that I say that my dear, is that it's the f'ing truth. Men don't want someone their own age."

"Well, I couldn't disagree more. Mark and I are the same age. I think the men we should want to be around are the ones who have a brain and want to engage in meaningful conversations with women, and that means somebody in their same generation."

"Well, that all sounds good, but you're naïve if you think it actually works that way. Anyway, he seemed a little weird. I can't quite put my finger on it, but almost like someone who may have a strange fetish or enjoys a little butt play." She was feisty today.

"Yup, just your type," I said, giggling. "Let's get out of here. My level of humiliation for one day is at ten."

The weeks went on like this for a while. We were in a routine: I picked her up, Winnie attempted to rip my clothes, we drove to the mall, we walked our two to three miles, blindly passing the same old Victoria's Secret, Banana Republic, Leather Loft, and very fattening food court. Sometimes she would become a little tired and get involved in a conversation with a fellow walker and I would leave her to finish the route. She had some friends there, so it seemed less sad to me and more that it was a healthy environment. There was a fair amount of socializing, and it was good for her. It made me happy to see her chatting with the Mantastics or hanging out in front of Ann Taylor while catching up with the lady with her red hair pulled up tight in a huge bun. She was convinced this lady had been a stripper or a prostitute, so I'm sure that's what she was always subtly trying to find out when they spoke. When we were back in the car, she downloaded the updates with a great amount of sarcasm and humor.

"Can you believe she is trying to pass off that hair color as natural? I'm not sure that shade was ever FDA approved. She keeps inviting me to come to the Whispering Pines Retirement Village.

They have a speed-dating event on Tuesday night, which seems like an oxymoron."

My mom was hilarious without really trying. Mostly it was because she said things that you just did not expect.

Chapter 3
The Trio

"WHEN IS THAT LITTLE BRAT of a granddaughter coming back for a visit?" Mom asked as I dropped her off in her driveway one day. "It has been almost two weeks since we've heard from her. I really miss her."

"Oh, I meant to tell you. I talked to her on Tuesday night. She's looking at dates to have us come out for a visit."

My daughter, Kylie, was twenty-five years old and living in Denver. She had been there for two years after graduating from college. She went there with her boyfriend, Connor, and they absolutely loved everything about it. I knew that she would probably never come back to Michigan, and I had started to try to accept that fact. My mom, on the other hand, had not. The three of us had been a tight trio ever since Kylie was born. She was the first grandchild. When I was single, post-divorce, we traveled a lot together. I tried to take them on at least one nice trip a year, and we always had a great time. I really wanted them to have an amazing bond, and they did. We got into some ridiculous situations and laughed and talked until we were hoarse. It was crazy that three women decades apart in age could have so much fun. We involved people we met along the way in dance contests, drinking games, and many, many ridiculous conversations.

One time, we were in a tavern in Sedona, Arizona, on a slow Sunday evening and we had the whole place involved in a conversation about soulmates. The sun was setting, and the colors that reflected off the red rock formations visible from the windows were spectacular. Every shade of orange, scarlet, and purple was out there, but not even that could distract us from the group conversation inside. There were some unlikely participants, like cowboys and truckers, and the discussion became more ludicrous as the night went on. Of course, Mom had to be the one who was convinced that there *is* such a thing as a soulmate in this world. She argued that there is one person who is perfectly right for everyone. You just need to move heaven and earth to find that one.

A guy in a cowboy hat, boots, and a shearling-collar jean jacket took the bait and argued his points of impossibility. "Well, I like your thoughts, but let's just consider a few things here, ladies. First off, this would require extensive world-wide travel for anyone to ever find this soulmate and most folks don't get too far outside of where they live for most of their lives. Also, what if your soulmate meets with an unfortunate accident or terminal disease before you meet them and dies? Are you just screwed? And finally—and this might be happening more and more these days—what if before you get a chance to find them, they decide to turn over to the gay?"

"These are great points, mister, and we'll consider them in the final verdict of this oh-so-important topic," I responded.

"Yes, suddenly deciding to be attracted to another sex is a potential wrinkle in the outcome," Mom thoughtfully added, biting her tongue, holding back the laughter.

He tipped the brim of his hat and got off the barstool to head to the men's room. We burst out laughing as he rounded the corner. Kylie spit up her drink.

A young brunette stopped our laughing session when she lifted her head from staring into her glass and said somewhat angrily, "The whole belief that someone is your soulmate just leaves you expecting too much from the relationship. I had high hopes that my last boyfriend was my soulmate and after he quit calling me and broke up in a text, my hopes fell apart. I guess that's why I'm stuck here instead of back at Arizona State. Not only am I heart-broken, but I'm sure that my parents are going to kill me." She then went right back to staring into her glass, and the silence was deafeningly sad. Hello, Debbie Downer. Clearly, we needed to move on to other contributors.

A local lady sitting on another barstool wanted to get in on the debate. "Well, I met my soulmate, so I know it's true."

My mom was so excited to find a supporter. "I knew there would be someone who understands what I'm talking about! Tell us!" she shouted.

"Well, we met many years ago and it was an instant connection. The energy was undeniable. We both felt a powerful draw and attraction—it was like we had known each other before, like a past-life connection. I know it sounds corny, but it was really like that for us. I always described it like coming together was bigger than just the two of us, and most of the time we knew what each other was thinking and feeling. It was the most amazing relationship of my life." She paused and took a sip of her rum and coke.

My mom immediately got excited to bring this great revelation to a close. "Wow, that sounds right for soulmate connections," she said, like she was some renowned expert. "How long have you guys been together?"

The woman casually replied, "Oh, we're not together. I found out he'd been sleeping with my best friend for years."

The place went crazy and we bought everyone involved a round of shots, even the depressed coed.

Kylie tried to introduce my mom to countless men that we encountered on our adventures. She had a personal challenge to find Mom a mate because she hated to think of her alone all the time. On another girls' trip, we were sitting in a restaurant in Chicago and my mom pointed out an attractive man walking in a park across the street. We were there for a long weekend of shop-ping, dining, and generally having a great time. Kylie got up from the table and went outside to speak to him. Of course, Kylie is attractive and can get a man to do just about anything, so she brought him into the restaurant to meet her "friends." Once Mom realized he was coming in, she slid down from the booth, practically army-crawled across the room to escape out the back door. We looked around and she was gone, and we were left with this poor guy who had no idea what was going on—the definition of awkward. We talked to him for a few minutes and then made an excuse to leave to meet up with Mom on the next street corner. We laughed so hard when we found her. What a crazy lady! Come to find out, he made toupees for men, so I guess my mom had a premonition about that one.

After a bit of back and forth via phone calls and emails, we settled on the upcoming Mother's Day weekend to make the trip to Denver. I called my sister, Jenny, to see if she could join us, as she was often in need of a mini vacation.

"Grab your ass, Jen, we are stealing you for a girls' trip with me and Mom! Can you get away for three days to Denver over Mother's Day weekend?"

"That sounds great! It'll take some planning but as long as I get the kids situated with rides to school, rides to volleyball, track and soccer, pickups from other after-school stuff, dentist appointments rescheduled and meals figured out, I can make it happen. Piece of cake. Hell yes, I'm in."

She had four kids who were extremely active with private school, activities, and sports, and Jen was busy all day, every day. She often described her life as an organized disaster, mostly a "clusterfuck." She was a great addition to our trio when she could escape.

Kylie lived in an upstairs apartment in a beautiful old Victorian house near the capital district in downtown Denver. The house was terra cotta-colored brick with turquoise and white trim situated on a street of painted lady Victorians. It looked very picturesque, but the location was another story.

"Ky, the house looks great. Did your landlord recently touch up the paint?"

"Yup, he's been doing a good amount of improvements lately. I think he's hoping if the house looks better, we won't find as many homeless people sleeping in the front landscaping. It doesn't seem to be working though, since Rocko sniffed out a sleeping guy over in that hedge during our morning walk last Wednesday."

"Oh my God, Ky, don't tell me stuff like that, it's not what a mother wants to hear."

"They're harmless, and I just won't tell you. Not really. I'll still tell you because it's fun to see your reaction." Of course, everyone laughed; they were always amused by Kylie bothering me.

I did find some consolation in the fact that she didn't live alone. Connor was also from Michigan and a great guy. He looked like someone who had just stepped out of an *Esquire* ad for Ralph Lauren cologne. He had a classic look but roughed it up with a slight beard and sharp green eyes. My mom often said that she would "like to keep him in a jar on a shelf in her kitchen." We didn't know exactly what that meant but decided it was best not to read too much into it. Kylie thought it was funny and she even told Connor, who laughed nervously.

"I have a plan for the next few days but want to see if it all makes sense to you guys. We can do anything you want, but this is what I thought: We can go out to our favorite Mexican restaurant around the corner tonight, and then after breakfast tomorrow, we can take a trip to Estes Park with a stop along the way at a winery. Dinner could be anywhere tomorrow night, and then I thought we might go to the Coors Brewery on Sunday and have a relaxing day before you head out Monday morning." Kylie paused to gauge our reactions, hoping we would be excited. The girl is a planner, it's in her genes, and she wanted to make this trip fun for us.

"I think that all sounds great, Ky. But I'm not sure Mexican food is the best option for Grandma's digestive tract. It could be an uncomfortable night for the rest of us." Jen whispered loudly and we all laughed.

"OK, screw you. I had one incident with Mexican food years ago and now I can't catch a break from you people," Mom said. "I think it sounds great, Ky."

After a fun first night at the neighborhood restaurant, we made plans to hit a winery the next day on the way to Estes Park. Mom and I piled onto the queen-sized bed in the guest room and Jenny slept on the pullout sofa. Kylie loved to entertain, and she had put together an impressive breakfast in the morning with waffles, fruit salad, eggs, and bacon. I helped set the table and spent a good amount of time looking for napkins, only to be informed that they were a complete waste since paper towels do the exact same thing. Millennials.

Connor left to gas up the SUV and returned with a small, wrapped package. Kylie informed us that it was from a dispensary down the street and contained a few pot edibles. Marijuana was legal in the state of Colorado and sold in small retail stores called dispensaries. Still a little unsure, we came closer to see the contents. One package was labeled Pop-Tart, and the other three looked like peppermint patties. We looked at each other, smiled, and gasped— "It's pot!" Kylie and Connor laughed at us and started to give us the details of the day's plan. The four ladies were going to share the Pop-Tart, and Connor would be the designated driver.

"Let's go for it!" Mom said. "You only live once, and this could be a riot."

I looked at Jenny and she nodded. We were all in.

"So, this is a small amount, and it may not do much of anything, but if it does, it will hit you in about 45 minutes. Hopefully, it will be a light, fun buzz and you guys will laugh a lot," Connor said.

He cut it into four pieces after talking through with Kylie the number of total grams in the Pop-Tart and dividing it by four. We all ate our piece, and it was surprisingly good. It tasted more like a smashed apple pie than a Pop-Tart. We headed out in the SUV with my mom in the front, and Kylie, Jen, and me in the back seat. It was a gorgeous day and the minute we left the city, the mountains captured our attention. The sun was shining, and the snow caps glistened with a sparkle that just seemed too beautiful to be random nature. The mountains cradled the highway in stony gray layers and occasional streams flowed where the water had decided to break through. Pine trees and bushes grew along the rocks, adding to the comforting, rustic feel. I understood every time I saw the landscape why we lost our sweet girl to that place.

The radio was playing Michael Bublé because that was what Mom requested, and we were singing along and enjoying the scenery.

Jenny suddenly turned to me and asked, "Are you starting to feel anything?"

"Not really, but I feel really happy, so maybe."

Just to be fair, none of us were virgins to marijuana, so it wasn't like we didn't know what to expect. Some had tried it in college, others at a few parties. Even Mom had been around a little pot in the past.

But somehow, someway, the dosage of this Pop-Tart crept up on us and over the next thirty minutes, we became completely stoned.

I looked at my mom in the front seat, and she was laughing hysterically at something that I said. "I have always thought that you were the funniest of all my kids."

"What the hell?" Jen said, laughing while lightly rapping her on the head from the back seat.

Kylie added, "Oh yeah, my mom is hilarious, that's all we need. Grandma, don't tell her that or we'll be dealing with it all day. I can't take her talking in that goofy Irish accent that sounds like she's from Long Island, not Dublin."

With that, I couldn't resist demonstrating, "Oh, now Kylie, you can shut the fuck up lassie."

And everyone busted out laughing because it was extra ridiculous. Yup, we were completely gone!

This nonsensical conversation with everyone talking at once went on for what seemed like an eternity, and I could not stop giggling sporadically. Kylie and I resorted to trying to hide under a blanket that we found in the back as we made up obscene lyrics to "Haven't Met You Yet." Even sober, Connor was entertained by this nonsense.

My mom kept saying, "It feels like there's dry ice on my head. We are never going to be able to get out of this car and face the public again. Ever!"

I looked over at Jenny, who had been laughing but had become suddenly quiet, and mouthed, "This is not good."

I, of course, laughed at her because the look on her face was funny. Sort of like a nun who just had their boob grabbed by the naughty boy in first-grade religion class. She looked surprised and concerned at the same time, but not amused.

"Sis, I'm sure it'll be fine," I mouthed back, still laughing.

We arrived at the winery and Connor pulled into a parking spot in a grassy lot. We were busy amusing ourselves with a discussion about my brother, Jeff, who we thought was a pre-hoarder. He kept a lot of mail stacked in various piles and saved the cardboard boxes from most items he purchased, so that was obviously pre-hoarding behavior. We wondered aloud if we should plan an intervention.

Connor announced that we had arrived, and we debated if we should get out.

Kylie and I swung the door open and marveled at the gorgeous surroundings. The winery was tucked alongside a mountain and had all sorts of wildflowers growing in rows along the parking lot edge with a sweet stone path leading to the winery's main doors. There was also a row of outer buildings to the left that contained the restrooms and a craft store. Jen and Mom were still in the vehicle.

"Hey, bitches, come on, this looks great. Let's go drink some WIIII-NE!" Kylie shouted.

"I need to go to the bathroom," Mom said, as she cracked open her car door. We all agreed that was a great idea. We were probably stalling, knowing that half of our group was not up to seeing people and the other half just didn't realize they shouldn't see people.

We headed to the restroom in the outbuilding, and on the path, we saw a cute black and white kitty. We all rushed up to the cat and he got on his tip toes and arched his back along the fence. We, of course, found this extremely adorable and emitted some high-pitched screams. We took turns holding and petting him, and even made up a name for the gorgeous black and white cat—Tuxedo, or Tux for short. Connor tore us away from Tux and tried to herd us toward the bathrooms. We let Mom go in first since she had the oldest and most fragile bladder. It was a one-stall bathroom, so we waited outside, giggling at various comments while Tux tried to get some additional attention. Mom was in there for what seemed like hours and Jen knocked on the door as we gathered closer. No answer.

"Mom, are you doing OK?" We heard this low giggle that then started to escalate into a full-on hysterical laugh as she slowly opened the bathroom door. When she had it open all the way she doubled over in a full howl and slammed it shut right in our faces. We were all laughing hysterically and really didn't know what the hell was happening.

"Mom, are you coming out? We are going to pee ourselves," I said.

"I may not be able to face the wine-tasting people—and I wet my pants a little—we just need to get out of here!" she said while giggling.

And with that, we finished our business, loaded up, and headed back down the mountain to the house. Chatting and laughing all the way.

After taking a three-hour nap to sleep it off, we emerged feeling less groggy. All of us were famished: after a good marijuana buzz, you need food. "Olive Garden sounds great to me right now. I'm sure you have one around here, Kylie." Mom suggested her favorite place, which was always Olive Garden.

Kylie said, "With all due respect, Grams, after a day like today, we are definitely not going to Olive Garden. Sorry, but this is my town and I'm taking you guys somewhere amazing."

We had a great dinner at Ocean Prime and spent the rest of the night roaming among bars along charming streets strung with Edison bulbs and crowds of happy, buzzed people. The edible situation was never brought up again for several months. My sister had remorse and wished we would have thought it through a little more thoroughly before jumping right into the situation. Her experience was not on the same level as ours. She wondered what her kids would think and went too far down that rabbit hole. My mom thought it was crazy fun, as did Kylie and I. Whenever we brought it up among just the three of us, we had a good laugh reminiscing. Connor felt terrible that he got the dosage wrong and realized his math error after it was too late. Jenny made it a point to ask the entire itinerary of an event before she committed to attending in the future. Smart.

Chapter 4
The After-Stops

ANOTHER ELEMENT of our daily routine that evolved over time was the after-stops. Mom was a big proponent of extending an activity into multiple stages before it was over. If we went on a mall walk, then we had to go somewhere afterward for coffee or tea or sometimes breakfast. If we had coffee or tea, then why not make a quick stop at a greenhouse or a florist shop? If we had breakfast, maybe just a run into Home Depot, Lowe's, or Target for one little thing. If we went to mass on Sunday morning, let's just stop for a pastry or go to a movie. She had a very subtle way of just moving me into the next activity and before I knew it, half the day was gone. There was a certain energy that just propelled me forward into what was next because it always sounded—and was— fun. I know now that it was her way of spending more time with me without making a big deal out of it. Kind of like an unbelievably soft sales pitch with an assumptive close. She just assumed that I wanted to do it, and so I did. I was usually the driver, so it's not like there was a gun to my head. I could have gone home at any time, but most days, I happily submitted.

Most of the after-stops involved flowers or plants in the spring, summer, and fall months. Mom loved flowers and was a very accomplished gardener. When you called her house in the summer, the phone just kept ringing. She didn't answer it because she was gardening. She spent hours in her yard pruning, planting, mowing, and weeding her beautiful flower gardens. The largest gardens were in the back of the house and took up the entire yard. They were cottage-style gardens and filled with flowers of all kinds: perennials and some annuals, shrubs, flowering trees, and statuary. There were also benches, arbors, and wind chimes from our travels scattered throughout. The gardens were unrestrained and wandered freely, cascading into each other in colorful abandon. She had worked on them a little bit every year since buying the house fifteen years earlier.

She had been describing her gardens one day while talking to a group at the mall. I left her because I really wanted to get the three miles in, and she was lollygagging. I overheard her mentioning to the group that she had been weeding her garden and it was currently filled with tulips and daffodils and their blooms reminded us that spring was here. I noticed that one of the gang standing there was Kent from the Mantastics. When I was done and met her on the benches in front of Saks about fifteen minutes later, she smiled and informed me that Kent was going to give her a ride home that day.

"Oh my God, look at you—you little slut," I whispered.

She laughed and told me that was rude and inappropriate, which was rich coming from her.

"We are just friends, and he wants to see the tulips." She said it like I would just let that go unchallenged.

"Oh, is that what we're calling it now? 'Seeing the tulips'?"

She slapped me on the arm, which she did a lot, and told me to "shut the F up."

"OK, have fun and call me right after so I can find out how he enjoyed seeing the tulips."

"Oh, he will love them," she said with a wink.

I got a call later that afternoon from a very relaxed Mom. "Hi Jule, I have to report that he has a passionate interest in flowers and horticulture overall, more than I was expecting."

"Or do you mean whore-ticulture! Oh wow, Mom, you're killing me. Please don't use any descriptions that include the words planting or cultivating!"

"Very funny. You asked me to call you, so that's what I am doing, but because I'm discreet, I'm not going to give you any gory details. However, I *will* let you know that it was a wonderful day and I'm thinking we will be seeing more of each other."

"So, you're going with this idea that you're a lady taking the moral high ground on this one, huh? Not sure that it fits, but I'll accept that considering that I don't need the details."

"OK great, I'm worn out anyway and plan to go catch a nap. I'll see you tomorrow for our walk."

I was excited for her since she hadn't had sex since before the turn of this century and it was about time! Poor Kent didn't have a chance, and I'm sure it was a lot to handle. Years of pent-up sexual tension coming at him with a backdrop of spring flowers and spiked lemonade. I imagine there were also little cookies involved. She creates quite a seductive scene.

The next time I saw Kent at the mall, he was smiling.

"Hey, ladies. How are you doing today?" he shouted from the other side of the hall as we passed them in the opposite direction. He was with the full Mantastics crew.

"Doing great, guys," I said.

We passed them another time and my mom stopped to chat. I kept walking. I liked to at least work up a sweat, or why bother? When I finally finished and caught up to her at Saks, she was chatting with Kent and another Mantastics member I have met before, named Frank.

"Hey, Julie, have you ever noticed how they pipe the scent from Cinnabon into the mall air system?" Frank asked. "It's so obvious that they are subconsciously trying to push diabetes-causing food in the morning. They might even be in cahoots with the medical industry. What do you think?"

We laughed, as he was very obsessed with this conspiracy theory, among others. Frank loved a good conspiracy theory.

"Well, it works on me. I just scarfed down two rolls on my last trip around," I said.

"Very funny, missy. Now you're just bragging because you and your mom don't pack on the pounds like the rest of us."

"Not true. I am a self-proclaimed fat ass."

"Where is the fat? You're in great shape," Frank added. They were always quick with a compliment.

"On that positive note, I have to get out of here. Mark wants me to look at some floor samples for our lower-level remodel. Mom, are you ready?"

"Sure, we better get going. See you guys tomorrow," Mom said and turned toward the doors, but moving a little more slowly than usual.

"You doing OK?" I said in her ear.

"Yes, just trying to get my bearings. Felt a little dizzy today."

"Probably because of all the strenuous activities with that guy," I said, tilting my head toward Kent, who was not paying attention.

"Jule, you are annoying."

When I got her into the car, my tone was a little more serious. "Are you sure you're feeling OK?"

"I'm sure I'm fine. Maybe getting a cold or something."

After I dropped her off, I reminded myself to bug her about setting a doctor's appointment. She was behind on her annual physical, and it was a good idea to get checked out. I was brought back to reality by a call from Kylie.

"Mom, it's over," she said between low sobs.

"Oh no, what happened?"

"Connor and I decided to call it quits. It just isn't working out."

"Oh sweetie, I know you've been struggling. I'm so sorry."

Fact is, they had been calling it quits on and off for the past month and it seemed inevitable. It turns out that opposites attract but can't always make the long haul. She always wanted him to be a little more aggressive in his career and make goals for the future. Connor needed someone who was a little more chill, and she was kind of a junior ball-buster.

"Yeah, it's just so hard. I wish it were different," Kylie said.

"Do you want me to come out? I could get there tomorrow." This is one of the benefits of still being unemployed—you are much more responsive in a crisis.

"No, I'm OK, but I'll need help soon since I plan to move out."

"He's staying in the apartment?" I asked.

"He's already moved in with his friend, Steve."

"When do you need to be out of there?"

"Our lease is up at the end of next month and I don't want to stay here, so I'm going to look for something else."

"Oh, sweetie, I can come out and help you."

"No, Mom, I would rather you come at the end of next month if that's OK. I could really use your help, but I think I should wait until next month."

"I don't know if I can hold off that long, but we'll see how it works out. I wish I were there to give you a hug. I love you so much, my girl."

"I know, Mom. It's just one of the sucky things in life that I have to deal with right now. I'll be OK. Please don't worry."

"Oh, you know I'll worry and will call or text you every hour."

"All right. Well, I'm not suicidal or anything, just heartbroken right now," Kylie said as she stopped her crying.

"Please call me if you need anything at all. I'm going to have to figure out a way to slip the news to Grandma. You know she's already named your children, pictured what they'll look like (secretly hoping for gingers), and decided how much they'll love her."

We both laughed because we knew it was true and that it would be hard for her to take the news.

I talked to Kylie six times that night and she seemed to be doing surprisingly well. It sounded like they were having a dispute over a few items but nothing major. It's not right when people at that age are so mature and reasonable.

The next day, I picked my mom up and we headed to the mall. She was in a good mood even though she said she'd slept restlessly. I also had a theory that had played out more than once: when Kylie was in distress, so was Mom. It was a very strange bond, and I had been aware of it for several years. When Kylie was first born, we lived about two hours away from my family. My mom always called me in the mornings and would let me know when she had a terrible night of sleeping, or should I say, not sleeping. These almost always correlated with me being up all night with a fussy baby.

Also, when Kylie first went away to college in Chicago, my mother was the one who guessed she was extremely homesick. She already knew that Kylie had cried herself to sleep a few nights before I heard about it. Ky had wanted to be in the dorm in downtown Chicago, but it was completely full. However, there was a room of four girls, and one would not be returning in the fall because her father had died. Ky took the spot without knowing any of the girls and immediately regretted the decision. They were cold and indifferent to her because they missed their friend. It was a long semester. My mom told me something was wrong, and I pried it out of Ky eventually. She had tried to spare me because she didn't want me to worry and hoped it would all work out. She ended up transferring rooms a few weeks later, and it did all work out eventually.

I needed to find a way to fill Mom in on the latest developments. I decided to just come out with it in the car, so we could talk it through on the walk and hopefully be over it by the time we headed to The Big Cup afterward for coffee.

"Mom, I talked to Kylie last night and it wasn't good news."

She slapped my arm while exclaiming, "Oh no, I knew it! What is going on?"

"Well, I know I mentioned she and Connor have been having some trouble. They've decided to call it quits."

"Oh no, is she OK? I had so many plans for them."

"I know, Mom, but this time, it is about them and not you," I laughed.

"Did that little ass Connor do anything to her?"

"No, they're just deciding to consciously uncouple … or whatever the hell they call it."

"Now that's some bullshit, Julie. It's better if they get pissed and maybe throw some stuff or post something mean on Bookit, or whatever people do now, but please don't be all civilized about it. That's unhealthy!"

"Well, I think you mean Facebook and that definitely would not help the situation. My goal is to have her get through this as best she can and then I'll go out and help her with the move and getting reorganized."

"And I'll go with you."

"Umm, OK, I guess."

And that was all there was except a few comments about getting him out of the jar on her shelf and Kylie being too good for him and that she will be fine, and do you want to check out the sale at Macy's after coffee? We called Kylie during lap two and checked in on her via voicemail; although that was most likely a complete waste of time because she told me she never listens to voicemails, and that no one her age ever does. They will call back if they see you called but they prefer email or just a text. Millennials.

As it turned out, we didn't need to go rescue the little sweetheart. She worked through the breakup and found a place on her own. She moved in with a girlfriend whose parents had just purchased a rental in Denver as an investment. I was really impressed: this might have been the first time that I witnessed her being so independent. The move to Denver had turned her into a grown woman who was now "adulting" like a pro. Although it made me feel less needed, I was proud of her.

Chapter 5
The Summer

MY FATHER HAD A LOVE AFFAIR with his boat "The Skate." It was a thirty-four-foot motor yacht with a kitchen, bathroom, main salon area, and master cabin. He purchased it new right after the divorce from my mother, and it was his version of starting a new life as a bachelor.

A little background: My parents got a divorce after twenty-eight years of marriage. It makes you wonder how a couple could be together that long and then just suddenly split up. They had their disagreements over the years like most couples, but none of us expected a divorce. When I was about seven years old, there was a knock on the door from a flower delivery man. He was bringing a huge vase of flowers from my dad for my mother. There were gorgeous white roses, baby's breath, purple statice, and her all-time favorite, huge, sweet-smelling lilies. She thanked the man, took the flowers, quietly closed the door, and then promptly and violently threw them against the wall. She turned and left the room without a word. After adjusting to what I'd just witnessed, I picked them up and took them into my bedroom since I thought they were still beautiful although a little smashed. I put whatever I could salvage into an old vase on my dresser. She never mentioned the flowers to me or my dad. The cause of that act of aggression—well, it's the age-old answer: infidelity. My father was what you would call a womanizer. A loveable womanizer, but a womanizer, nonetheless. I guess you must be loveable to be a womanizer, or you wouldn't attract the women. My mom was mostly unaware of the extent; she knew it in hindsight but not so much during the marriage. Dad had a great job as an executive in the automotive industry, had many admirers, and traveled a lot. This combination of factors was what potentially led to the dalliances. Maybe he was a believer in the "what happens out of the country doesn't count" theory. As the years went by, he started to get sloppy, and one day years later, my mom opened the trunk of his car and found a woman's tennis bag. It obviously wasn't hers because she never played tennis.

That started the wheels in motion of a three-year-long divorce process where words flew like missiles and we were often caught in the crossfire. They had a good amount of assets that needed to be divided. At the time, my sister Jenny was fourteen and the only one still at home. The rest of us—my two brothers, Jeffrey, and Jonathon, and I—were either at college or newly graduated and starting jobs. It was not a great time, and even after the divorce was final there were still hard feelings throughout the family. Jenny had the worst situation because she was with Mom during the week and Dad every other weekend. The older kids ignored most of the back-and-forth and tried not to take sides, but we still silently suffered. It took many years before Mom would even mention his name. We often did not tell her if we spent time with him because it really upset her to think we were "letting him off the hook." We just wanted to stay out of it because you never really know what goes on in a marriage, even with your own parents. But as time passed it got easier to communicate, and finally last year we made the deal with him to buy the boat.

Summers in Michigan, the Great Lake state, are glorious, and boats allow us to take full advantage of the water. This is mostly because we endure cold, rain, and snow almost eight months out of the year, so the four good ones are truly inspiring. We are outside as much as we can be and try to grill, boat, swim, tan, picnic, and play sports as much as possible. When my dad told the family he would be selling it, Mark and I jumped at the chance to make it ours. It worked out perfectly for us, and we kept it at a marina in Grand Haven, a beautiful coastal town on Lake Michigan.

Mark and I spent our weekends there and had many friends at the marina. The boat could sleep up to six people, but we always had more than that during the Fourth of July weekend. It was our sanctuary, and we were glad that my dad had offered to sell it to us when he decided it was time to quit boating. There was just one catch: since he gave us a great price, we had to let him use it on the weekends we were not going to be there. This seemed like a fair exchange until we heard from some of our marina neighbors.

Our friends recounted with amusement that he was having a really good time out there and that he brought different women each weekend he used the boat. The standard profile seemed to be about twenty years younger, good looking, and somewhat light on intelligence. I only add the last part because of conversations that were relayed to us by some of our marina neighbors. For example, one of the women was chatting with our slip neighbor, Amy, and had the following exchange:

The woman (calling her Dumb Brunette): "I just love it out here. It's so pretty with all the different kinds of boats."

Amy: "Yes, it's especially nice to see all the sailboats out on the water, especially when they have races and regattas."

Dumb Brunette: "Oh yes, but it's too bad that they can only take their boats out when it's windy. That's a lot of wasted time just sitting in the marina."

Amy: "Umm no, sailboats also have motors."

Also, there were cases of mistaken identity when a marina friend yelled my name to one of the tall blonde dumbasses at the pool. I mean, it was from far away, but still, the ultimate in "gross" is being mistaken as your dad's weekend bimbo.

He called me one Monday, "Hey Jule, if you and Mark are out at the boat this week, can you check around for a piece of lost jewelry?"

"Sure, Dad. What exactly did you lose?" (He never wears jewelry.)

"Oh, it's a necklace."

"A necklace. A necklace, huh. Well, what does it look like?"

There was a pause and it sounded muffled like he was holding his hand over the receiver.

"It's a gold chain with a dolphin charm and a little diamond for the eye."

"Well, that sounds really precious, Dad. I'll look for your necklace when we get out there Thursday night," I said in a sarcastic tone.

"Great, thanks, darlin'."

I never found it, but I was creeped out imagining the kinds of activities that were taking place on our innocent weekend retreat. Mark just laughed and said, "That's your dad; you already knew that."

He was out of control, but we mostly pretended not to notice as that was the deal on the boat. Also, it was the entertainment for the marina folks: most of them didn't have cable TV.

In the summer months, my mom and I started to walk outside at a local park. It was a beautiful place with a small, picturesque lake and wooded areas. There were paths and bike trails so there was a lot of variety for walking. Some of the friends from the mall like Lorri, Kent, and Frank often joined us, as well as crazy Winnie. Winnie loved all the smells and often kicked up a squirrel or rabbit. This would send her sprinting after it, jerking Mom's arm off with the leash. This, in turn, would provoke a super shrill, "Winnie, you idiot!" from my mom. It was a choreographed dance they did together, and both seemed to understand their roles. I did worry that one of these days this dance would turn into a tumble and maybe even a drag, but Mom was adamant about her devotion to Winnie.

"This poor puppy was mistreated early on, and I'm going to do everything I can to make sure she has a great rest of her life."

It seems that meant no discipline to make her life extra special.

I did notice that my mom was spending more time sitting at a picnic table chatting than walking. I asked her about it on our way home one day. "Mom, are you sick of walking, or just more interested in the chit-chat?"

"I know I've been slacking off lately, but my knee has been giving me a little trouble and I'm sure it's from that fall I took on the ice a few years ago."

"Oh yeah, I remember that fall. You could still have some damage."

It sounded like something she should go see her doctor about, but after all my nagging, she still made excuses. She was getting older, and I told myself not to expect her to always keep up with me. She was really enjoying the time outside and talking with friends. It supplemented her alone time in her flower garden and charity work at the church. She volunteered to help with the church food bank and delivered holiday baskets to families. When she first mentioned the idea of volunteering, she told my sister, Jenny, and me that she had asked the priest if she could use her volunteer time to work with the prisoners at the county jail. We were astonished and thought she must just be testing us to see if we are really listening.

"Mom, what the hell are you thinking, asking to work with prisoners?" Jen said.

"You do realize they're in jail for a reason, right?" I asked.

"Oh, you guys, it's something I've always wanted to do and I feel like I could help them as someone to not only talk to but really listen to them. Many of them don't have support from the outside."

"A lot of the time there's a good reason for that. Mom, you could be attacked, or even raped!" I said.

"You girls are overreacting, but at least I'd have a good story to tell at the next family reunion."

We never knew if she was serious or just trying to get a reaction. But the priest had the good sense to say no to her request, so now she was organizing carb-heavy food baskets for needy families instead of counseling violent prison inmates.

That summer was also the point where Mark and I hit a few bumps in the road. He didn't think it was healthy for me to be so out of touch with the business world. I think a lot of his complaints centered on a little jealousy that I had so much free time while he was working ten-hour days as his consulting business continued to grow. And maybe he was concerned because I had come to know all the ladies' names on the *Real Housewives* series on Bravo. I gave him my full synopsis one night at dinner on the perils of Andy Cohen starting to fill the cast with B-list actresses and how it seemed like a Hail Mary to keep the shows relevant. I had a whole theory on the potential downward spiral if they couldn't keep the cast interesting and just substituted with actors. Mark seemed unimpressed with my wealth of *Real Housewives* analysis and knowledge.

One thing was true: I didn't miss the corporate struggles. Maybe that's why I watched the ladies fight for screen time on reality TV. It felt familiar. Mark didn't seem too upset; he always concluded our discussion with an, "I don't care what you do, I just want you to be happy." I was happy and surprisingly fulfilled with loving my family, feeling completely present in my life, and relaxing with the *Housewives*.

It was refreshing not to be exhausted or worrying about department budgets and revenue goals. I also noticed that I had stopped sweating under my arm so much, which was obviously a stress-related issue. It was amazing how quickly you can adapt to a new pace of life and feel so content. But he had a point because I *did* feel the need to work on something interesting. I had been considering an idea for a mobile application that could really help people. To get started it would need input from a finely tuned focus group. Luckily for me, I had the perfect group in mind.

Chapter 6
The Goods

I WENT OVER TO MOM'S HOUSE and the outside door was open, but the screen door was locked, which was unusual. When I knocked, Winnie came running with a legless koala toy dangling from her mouth as she jumped up and down.

"Where's Miss Suzy, Winzes?"

Of course, there was no response from her, so I knocked again. Mom slowly emerged from the hallway in her bathrobe with some wild hair and a dazed expression.

"Hey, Mom, did you forget that I was coming today?"

"Oh my gosh, I guess I did. What were we going to do?"

She moved Winnie aside with her foot and unlocked the screen door. I could tell that I had awakened her.

"No big deal. We were going to walk at the park and then go to the greenhouse to get a plant for Aunt Karen's birthday."

"Oh my God, I can't believe I forgot that. I slept really sketchy last night so I must have overslept once I did fall asleep around 4:00 a.m." She was now in the kitchen staring blankly into a cabinet.

"Sorry if I woke you, Mom. We can do this another day, no big deal."

"Let's have some coffee because I have to tell you about a funny dream that I had." She was now fully awake and seemed to be easing into a good mood, so I decided to stay and chat for a bit.

Her dreams were entertaining, so it was worth the time.

"OK, can't wait to hear this one," I said.

She settled for a cup of hot coffee doctored up with vanilla cream and I had one as well. We went into the living room and she sat on the leather couch while I plopped down in a club chair. Winnie of course had to horn in and jump onto the couch, spilling a little bit of my mom's coffee. "Oh, Winnie!"

Mom took a few sips. "In the dream, we were back in the house in Rustic Hills. But it was out of whack time-wise because you were in high school."

We lived in Rustic Hills when my dad was going through several promotions, and we landed in Ohio for two years before we moved back to Michigan during my freshman year of high school. I wasn't welcomed in the popular group. I had spent nine years in private schools as we moved around for my father's corporate climb. When you are young, you don't realize what it's like to be popular. I was motivated by classes and learning, and the private Catholic schools I'd gone to until this point offered that aplenty. I had won the essay contest, the science fair, and numerous other academic awards. I completed my homework every night and took great pride in my grades.

With this last move, I was determined to go to a public high school. I pleaded with my parents and used the guilt trip about not knowing anyone in this new town. In my sales pitch, I mentioned that this way I would at least get to know the neighbor kids, even though we now lived in a very snooty neighborhood called Highland Ridge and the kids seemed somewhat eccentric. Their parents were entrepreneurs, executives, doctors, and lawyers. At the high school, I was an ostracized nerdy girl during my freshman year. My friends were other girls who liked science and took pre-college courses. I was so bored with the curriculum because I had already studied those exact topics in seventh grade, so I started looking for other things to occupy my time. This was the point where I decided to try out for cheerleading to meet some new friends. I didn't make the squad because of a severe inability to do the splits, but the experience opened a whole new world for me. I spent lots of time on the phone and was invited to after school shopping and weekend parties. I quickly established a close group of fun friends.

Mom sipped her coffee and continued, "Anyway, in the dream, you came into the house with three of your high school friends and asked to use the car. The girls were from that little group you hung around with all the time in high school. What did you guys get called, I can't remember?"

"Oh my God, Mom—you mean The Goods!"

We both started laughing at this complete blast from the past. I couldn't believe that I remembered the name we'd earned, but there it was, right in the front of my brain just when I needed it.

"Yeah, The Goods! What a bunch of crazy idiots. But wow—you girls were cuties," Mom remembered.

"Looking back, that was such a fun time! You know we had a reputation for getting the party started whenever we went. Everyone wanted to sit at our table in the commons and hang out with us on Saturday nights, or at least that's what we all thought," I added, and actually felt stupid saying it as an almost fifty-year-old woman.

Surprisingly, there was quite a bit of diversity in our group of eight. We had smart girls, crazy girls, slutty girls, and funny girls. I became cemented in this group sophomore year because I could make people laugh. Also, I was cute enough and had a decent wardrobe, which were the main two prerequisites. We had nicknames that were the result of some rationale that made more sense when we were drinking and giggling. I was dubbed "Juice" during powderpuff football practice in the fall of junior year. I was always a tomboy and loved playing fullback because I could run with the ball. So, as girls who didn't do well with sports references, I became Juice. It was unfortunate that later my namesake became a cold-blooded killer ... allegedly.

"Remember when you busted me and read all the notes from my friends? I came home from school one day and you had them spread out on the kitchen table."

"You girls were always up to something, and I considered it my duty as a responsible parent to know what was going on."

"Or you were just bored and needed a little excitement, so you decided to search my room to get some contraband and bust me."

"That may have been part of it, but you have to admit, Julie, you were very disrespectful when you referenced me, and most of the notes were pretty stupid."

We both laughed, and I agreed with her because it was true. You could wind up receiving up to six notes a day from various Goods members and the topics were always along a few themes: what are we doing tonight or this weekend, why is X not talking to me, where did X get that hideous outfit, what are we wearing to X event, and why is X (not a Good of course) such a slut? For example:

Hey Juice—
Last hour I told Mike S. if he comes to my party tonight to keep his delinquent friends under control. Ask your mom again if you can come— you can't possibly still be grounded. How long has it been this time? Tell her I will get you home when you want. I really need you there because I am afraid that something will happen (Bad). What the hell did Scuzzy Kelly say to you? Is she sleeping over? I hope not. I do hope that Toad can make it though, she is too funny. You better work it out and be there—handle Suzanne! I'm in typing class right now and there was an exercise and on the list was the word group and I typed groin. I am laughing so hard right now because I can't erase it. I am an ass.
Later—Minnie (FYI—Minnie was six feet tall and the star of our girls' basketball team.)

Hey Minnie—
I just walked to my locker and Toad was there, she's in. I also want BJ there cuz I miss her. I am dying with Mom's latest grounding b.s., it's gone

on over a week now and she is not breaking. I'll see if I can trade out some babysitting for my little sis to get off tonight. If I can go, what will we wear? Probably something warm since it's F'in cold. I think I will try to crimp my hair again—hopefully not burn it off. Also, we better win this game if we're going. I hope Mike does come to your party. He's fun. I have a test in Badra's class—I'm screwed. Stayed up late talking to Bill, did not study.

Later—Juice

Hey Juice—

You were making me laugh so hard in first hour. I couldn't stop. I thought Mrs. Miller was going to boot us. Are you doing anything at lunch? Is Fish Face here today? I haven't seen her yet. What's going on tonight? Where are you guys going up north this weekend? I'm so glad we don't have school. I guess Carol was telling Slusha (slut) about what she said to Mike and Tom H. overheard her and was getting really pissed. He told me that he hates her. Good!

Well, I guess T.K. isn't here today. Prob. screwing that guy from Handy H.S.

Just a shorty.

Later—Beefy (Beefy had a huge chest and ridiculously small waist.)

Hey Beefy—

I know, Miller seemed to be in a daze today which was good. I'm sitting in third hour with Fish Face right now, she seems like she is HIGH—ha-ha. She just looked at me because I laughed. I don't have any plans for tonight since Bill asked me to hang out and I kind of said OK. But I am maybe gonna change plans with him if I can get the car tonight. I'm not feeling the couple hangout. Rents are still deciding if I'm grounded from the car. I really want to go to those Central parties that we heard about from Jeff. If I can't drive, Kelly Scully will and she wants everyone to come. I think she and Min are doing OK now. That fight was stupid weird.

Let me know what you're going to wear since it may be outside.

Later—Juice

There was always some developing drama and much scholastic enrichment wasted on these notes. I still have a good collection of them stashed away. We should have been studying instead considering that only about five of the eight went to college. It was a precursor to my love of housewives-manufactured drama like an episode of TGBC, *The Goods of Bay City*, except without the face fillers and table flipping.

After establishing that The Goods were involved in this dream, my mom grabbed an afghan and continued with her story.

"So, when I told you the car was off-limits because you were grounded, you and your fellow Goods stomped off to the backyard."

"I was always grounded; it was so humiliating!"

"Yes, but you knew you deserved all of them, Julie." She looked at me and waited for my reaction. She knew that to this day I feel many of the groundings were without merit, but I didn't say anything more.

She continued, "I eventually stepped outside to see what you girls were doing, and this is where it gets foggy. You were all sitting by the pool in your bras and nothing else. I mean no pants on at all, sitting cross-legged in a circle. And Jule, this was well before waxing was in fashion—so you get the picture. Our neighbor, Mr. Hamidy, was also there with you girls. Do you remember him?"

"Who the hell could forget that guy? He was quite unforgettable! Remember he owned that medium-sized snack company that made potato chips, cheese puffs, and popcorn, and he was successful but eccentric. They always had the best snack selection at their house and the parents were never around, so it was fun. He walked his two Irish setters at all hours of the night around the neighborhood cul-de-sac. And the crazy outfits! My favorite was the nightshirt and matching stocking cap."

"Yes, Julie, I obviously remember since my subconscious conjured him up for this dream."

"I also remember that you and Dad thought he was an alcoholic or maybe had a pill problem but was still fun at neighborhood parties."

"Yes, yes, I remember. Do you want to hear this or not?" Suz was getting short with me.

"Well, Hamidy is just sitting there in a lounge chair wearing one of those nightshirts and a stocking cap. He looked up at me but didn't say anything. And the weirdest part was you were all playing that dice game, Yahtzee."

"Oh, that is the weirdest part—Yahtzee!" I laughed. "Not the fact that we are teenage girls sitting around sans pants with big bushes out and hanging with the creepy neighbor who is dressed like Ebenezer Scrooge!"

"I guess you're right, Jule." She was laughing now. "Where the hell do these dreams come from and what do they mean? Maybe I don't want to know what they mean. I might have some mental issues."

We continued reminiscing as we finished our coffee, and then she got dressed. We went to the greenhouse that day but not to the park for a walk. I could tell she wasn't feeling tip top. That was the first time that I got aggressive with her about seeing the doctor.

"Mom, I think you need to call Dr. Manning and get a checkup. When was the last time you saw her, anyway?"

"I saw her about eight months ago for my physical, and it was a weird visit."

"How so?"

"I just don't feel the same around her ever since she filled me in on her dating life. Remember when her husband passed a few years ago and I went to the funeral? He died suddenly from a heart attack. Which seems somewhat bad for her brand; after all, she's an MD. I felt so sad for her because it was such a shock. We started talking more and more when I went to see her for my appointments, and then she filled me in on her online dating escapades. There was some graphic info. She told me about a guy she was seeing, and it was uncomfortable. There I was, lying on the table getting a breast exam while she's telling me about fooling around with him in his car outside a Starbucks."

"It seems like a doctor would be a little classier than that. I mean, doing it in a car and at Starbucks—really?"

"Yeah, she was just happy to be getting some … she's not the most attractive woman."

"Meow! Do you think we need to find you a new doctor?"

"No, I'll call her, and you can go with me. Hopefully, she won't spill any sexcapades if you're there."

"Hopefully, she will." We both laughed.

Chapter 7
The MD

MY MOM ABSOLUTELY LOVED her birthday. It usually turned into a weeklong "Suz-abration." This included various lunches and dinners that culminated with the birthday crescendo: a picnic with her kids and grandchildren. We knew it was coming and that there was no use fighting it—Suzy loved a picnic. The best we could hope for was bad weather to get us out of it or cut it short with a sporadic squall. I broached the subject with her on our way to the park one morning in late August.

"Mom, your birthday's right around the corner, so I wanted to get the annual picnic planned. You know everyone is waiting with bated breath to get the details."

"I get the sarcasm, Jule. I know you all hate the picnic."

"That's probably why you insist on doing it every year, right, Mom? Just a little torture for the family?"

"There may be something to that, but contrary to popular opinion, I do really enjoy it."

"OK, so who do you want to invite this year? Obviously, all your kids and the grandkids. Do you want to see if Lorri and Kent could make it, and maybe even your brothers and sisters?"

"I'm good on Lorri and Kent, but hell no to the brothers and sisters."

"Wow, I guess that's a firm 'no' then."

"Oh, Jule. I have to confess something to you, and you're not going to like it."

"Uh-oh. What did you do?"

"Well, it started innocently enough. Your Aunt Karen asked me to go to a sisters' lunch with her and Marty a few months ago and I declined. I told her that I had to work and couldn't make it."

"What the hell are you talking about? You haven't worked since you retired eight years ago."

"Then why do they think I'm handing out mini wontons and all-natural guacamole samples at my local Costco store?"

"What? So, you faked a job to get out of having lunch with your sisters?"

"Well, 'faked' is a strong word. You remember that I *did* apply for that job last year because I wanted something to do and never heard from them. So, it's possible that I could be working there. Although in hindsight, the job is not great since there are always greedy kids with no adult supervision and a lot of being on your feet all day... Maybe I need to rethink this job idea."

"Mom, it's not a real job! This is a new low for you, I'm actually shocked."

"Yup, Jule, I did it, and now I must keep up the charade so they don't catch onto the lie."

"I can't believe that you have the balls to lie like that to your family. What if I did that to Jenny someday, how would you feel?"

"I wouldn't care because I would think that you had a good reason to avoid her."

We both laughed because the whole thing was ridiculous and we both knew she would be livid if I did that to my sister. She always wanted her kids to be close but then distanced her own siblings.

"I just don't understand why you're always so down on your family."

"You know there are a lot of issues from our childhood that we just ignore, and I am sick of it. I would rather not see them than put up with the bullshit." She was now venting. Here we go, wading into the childhood pond. I didn't feel like getting in there with her, so I gave in on the invite question.

"OK, I won't invite them, but I won't lie about this ridiculous fake Costco job. I hope they don't ever ask me about it. Although, it *is* kind of funny to picture you giving out food samples to the masses on Saturdays, wearing a smock and a hairnet."

I finished the topic of the picnic. It was always the same plan: We meet at Deer Lake Park under the pavilion. We decorate with helium balloons, flowers in vases, and bright tablecloths. Mark makes ribs and chicken. I make her favorite potato salad. I also make the coveted Raspberry Dream cake. I invented this cake because my family couldn't get enough buttercream frosting and raspberries. My brothers, Jeff and Jon, bring beer and wine. (We can't make it through the picnic without the booze.) Jen makes snacks and a huge salad since she insists on us having one at all family events. Maybe to try and balance out the enormous amounts of buttercream frosting. We play bocce ball and fly kites. If it's warm enough, we let the little kids swim. My mom loved the consistency and comfort of the picnics.

So, we were all set. Now I just needed to get my siblings to show up in two weeks without too much complaining.

"Oh, I forgot to tell you that I got a hold of Dr. Manning's office and I have an appointment next week."

"Perfect, Mom, I'll go with you—what day?"

"Tuesday at 2."

"OK, I'll pick you up on Tuesday at 1:15."

"Just watch, with you there, she'll probably be completely professional."

"Hopefully, you'll ask her if she's still dating that guy so we can liven up the appointment."

"I'll see if it fits into the conversation, Jule."

We showed up at Dr. Starbucks Parking Lot the next Tuesday. The office had been updated since I had been there with Mom the previous year, and it was a huge improvement. The carpet was new and was a light gray with a modern textured pattern. The chairs had been replaced with ones with subtle mint green leather upholstery and dark-stained wood arms. They had also replaced all the mismatched artwork on the walls with tasteful black and white prints. Magazines that used to be scattered everywhere were now in baskets at the end of each row of chairs. It looked like they had some help: it seemed to be a professional job. The only things that remained and seemed out of place were the two front windows in the reception area. One was labeled with big letters for check-in and the other with check-out. This didn't seem to work with the new sophisticated style, but they must have decided it was functional, so it stayed. I went to the check-in window and let them know that my mom was there.

Tracy, the regular nurse, called my mom into the exam area and I went with her. It was a spartan beige room with three cabinets and an exam table and some basic instruments. This is where the budget must have run low during the redesign.

"Suzanne, so great to see you. How are you doing?"

"Hey, Tracy. Good to see you. I am trying to shut up my daughter, so I agreed to have a checkup. I think you've met Julie."

"Yes. Hi, Julie. Sometimes we need to nag our parents to get them to take care of themselves. Are you having any issues, Suzanne?"

"Maybe a few little things, but they could be just old age stuff. You never know what's normal at this age or something to worry about. Getting older is not a great time, Trace."

"Oh, I know, Suzy. I'm feeling it sometimes myself. Let's get your chart updated and then I'll get Dr. Manning in here."

Tracy weighed her and commented, "Are you trying to lose weight? Because I'd like to know your secret. Down fifteen pounds is fantastic."

"I've been walking a lot and it's helped me take off a few pounds."

"That's good! I've tried everything with no results. We can all stand to lose a few pounds to keep our heart and joints in good shape," Tracy said robotically like she'd read it in a nurse's magazine.

She also took Mom's blood pressure and temperature, and quickly clicked the keys of her laptop to enter the info. "Dr. Manning should be right in. Good to see you."

A few minutes later, the doctor walked in and immediately gave my mom a hug. "Great to see you, Suzy. How have you been?" Dr. Manning was about sixty-two years old and what you would call a "handsome" woman. She wasn't traditionally pretty but was attractive in a matter-of-fact sort of way. Her features were strong, she had good posture, and she exuded confidence, like Sigourney Weaver or Glenn Close. She had on a white coat over a navy-blue pantsuit with small gold hoop earrings. She wore her hair in a sleek bob, and it was honey-blonde. Her features were plain, and the makeup was minimal but well done. It seemed that she paid attention to her appearance and tried to make the most of what she had to offer. I had met her before but had to stop looking at her because all I could picture right now was her in the backseat of a car, giving some guy head in a Starbucks parking lot. Snap out of it, Julie!

"Hi, Carol, great to see you, too. You remember Julie?" My mom and the doctor were apparently on a first-name basis.

"Oh yes. Good to see you, Julie." She shook my hand. We exchanged some other pleasantries and then Dr. Manning got down to business.

"Now, what brings you ladies in today?"

"Well, I've been having a few little things bothering me and I told Julie that I would get checked out. My sleeping has been kind of off, and I feel a little tired and disoriented sometimes when I haven't slept well. Also, I have had some knee pain that comes and goes."

Dr. Manning got up from her stool and listened to my mom's heart and looked in her ears and at her eyes with her device. She also tested her reflexes. Dr. Manning wrote while looking at the chart. She looked up and said, "I'm still getting used to the laptop and prefer to write in the chart. I really need to get used to that damn machine ... I see that you lost fifteen pounds. Tell me about that."

"I started walking earlier this year, and it has really helped. I'm also not eating as much junk."

"So, you've been walking more, and that may be why you have some knee pain. Didn't I give you a prescription for a mild sleeping pill at your last visit?"

"You did, but I really haven't been taking them. They make me feel drowsy in the morning."

"Well, Suzanne, I have to say you seem to be doing really well. Try the sleeping pills when you can get to bed at a decent time. You should have eight hours of sleep when you take one and then you shouldn't feel drowsy."

Just then my cell phone rang. Damn, I thought I'd turned it to vibrate. The number was familiar, so I excused myself and took it in the hall.

"Hi, this is Julie," I said, trying to sound like a professional.

"Hi, Julie. This is Brad Briggs from the Briggs Group. How are you today?"

Brad had called me a few weeks earlier to talk about potentially placing me back in the media world in an executive position. I'd told him it would really depend on the organization since I was trying to avoid companies that were still going through the digital bloodbath. He totally understood and said he would see if there was a fit that might make sense.

"Great, Brad, nice to hear from you. I'm actually at a doctor's appointment with my mother right now."

"No problem, I'll be quick. I just wanted to let you know that I have an opportunity for you and wanted to see what you thought of it. There is a progressive company headquartered in Dallas that is looking for a general manager. The company is Firefox Partners, and they currently have twelve newspapers and seven radio stations and are in the market to buy some television as well. They have great financials and will be expanding over the next year with local properties. This would be at the corporate level, and you could be in either Dallas or Chicago. They really want to add a woman for this position, and they like your background. Do you want to consider it by having a first discussion with them?"

"Wow, Brad, it sounds like they are in growth, which is good. Let me do a little research on them and we can talk in a few days?"

"OK, I'll send you the job description and information on the company."

I hung up and headed back into the exam room. They were laughing about something and wrapping it up. Oh no, I may have missed some new sexcapade adventures.

"OK, Suzanne, we'll see how you do with the sleeping pills and the vitamins and I will see you in six months. Call sooner if you need to. Nice to see you again, Julie."

Dr. Manning headed out and I looked over at Mom. "So, what'd I miss?"

"Oh, Jule, she was filling me in on her latest relationship and it got a little weird again. Apparently, she is quite an internet dating sensation. Guys are super interested in a doctor who is close to retirement. She has been going out with a stockbroker who is ten years younger than her. She mentioned that he takes Cialis, and they are having a great time exploring each other sexually. I'm not sure why she thinks I care, but I don't know how to get her to stop talking."

"Oh man, I wanted to hear that and missed it! It sounds like she's getting a lot of action. Good for Dr. Carol, but I really want to know what she said about you."

"Well, you'll be happy to know, she said I'm healthy enough to pick up an extra shift at Costco!"

"Very funny, Mom. We'll discuss this in the car."

We headed to the check-out window and sorted out the insurance stuff. On the way home, my mom recapped Dr. Manning's assessment and recommendations. It came down to normal aging, vitamins, and better sleep. The walking was great for her overall health but if her knee kept bothering her, she should call back. It sounded a little lame to me. But Mom seemed happy with the visit and was going to try the vitamins and sleeping pills. The problem would be finding a night when she could get to bed for a full eight hours of sleep. She was notorious for staying up until two in the morning doing who knows what. The lady was a night owl.

Chapter 8
The Idea

LATER THAT FALL, after a few discussions with Brad Briggs and the CEO of Firefox Partners, I declined the general manager position. I thought that I might be able to move to Chicago or even Dallas if the offer was good enough. Mark could handle most of his consulting clients from a remote location. But after long consideration and discussions with Mark and my mom, I knew we couldn't move. Something was happening with the bond in my family and particularly with my mother that I had never experienced before. We were uniquely tied together and needed each other every day. This was a feeling that was a little confusing to me and provided more comfort than any salary or job title. I needed to stay put and figure it out from here, plus I decided it might be time to take a big risk.

For a few months, I had been considering starting my own marketing firm and building a mobile application as the first product. The working concept of the app was called "Friendly Neighbors." The focus was to connect people who are looking for flexible work schedules (called Partners) to solve the basic household needs of our aging or single-household population (called Clients). The Clients are the ones who would pay based on a subscription service. The idea is very retro—like being able to ask your close neighbors for help with simple, everyday problems. The needs could range from changing hard-to-reach light bulbs to more complex tasks like going to the grocery store or meal preparation or yard work ... there was a whole list of services that could be provided. There would be no medical services, and maybe at some point, we would add prescreened professionals to do light carpentry, electrical, or plumbing work, but those were not included in the startup model. I had it all laid out in a proposal document but needed to get some hard data before moving to the next phase. The Mall Walking Club was a perfect group to do a focus study since they fit the Client profile. I had mentioned it to Kent at the picnic, and he thought it was a great idea and wanted to help. We decided to get working on a focus group survey for next week.

The picnic had been the first time that I had some time to really talk to Kent between bocce ball games with my family. I grabbed us both a beer and sat down on the picnic table bench while my mom was down at the lake with the kids. "I'm really glad to see you and my mom having fun together. She can be a feisty handful most of the time."

"Oh no, we are actually having a lot of laughs hanging out together. My wife died ten years ago after a long battle with breast cancer, and I thought I would never meet anyone again after that loss. But your mom is quite something and keeps me guessing most of the time. She is an incredible lady."

"Oh, I'm sorry. I'm sure that was a hard time for your whole family."

"Yeah. I tried to take care of her myself, but it became too much, and we had to bring in some help. I found myself working more and more just trying to cope with it all. That's why I really count on the guys you see me walking with; they were always there for me. I worked with them for the last twenty years I was at Ford. Before I retired, I put in forty years in engineering and enjoyed every minute of it."

He started at Ford right out of college. He also alluded to a patent that he held in the automotive industry. It was something he developed about twenty years earlier, and it sounded like it had been extraordinarily successful for him. I didn't want to pry because he was noticeably guarded. He changed the subject and we talked about his kids and grandchildren before he got called into the next bocce game.

The following Monday morning, I went to pick up Mom to head to the mall. Winnie met me at the door as usual and proceeded to jump and lick me everywhere she could find skin. And if she couldn't find skin, she wasn't beneath just licking clothes. By now, she weighed about sixty pounds. She had slightly curly black and gray hair that my mom kept long and floppy. I always gave her attention because she was super cute and extremely loveable.

"Ahh, thanks, Wins. I appreciate the nice dog smell. Hey, Mom, are you ready to roll?"

"Hi, yes, I'm all set. Can you believe that we got a little snow last night?" she said as she came around the hall corner.

"Yup, the first one is always exciting and pretty until we get to January and we all want to cut ourselves."

"Oh, I know. For some reason, I'm not looking forward to this winter. I think it's going to be a bad one."

"You need to get your ass to Florida one of these days, and then you can just come back here for the summers."

"I would love that, and hopefully that'll be in my plan in the next few years."

We continued to talk about her options for Florida and her ongoing plans as we drove to the mall. We had been going to Sanibel Island on the Gulf for many vacations over the past twenty years. She also owned a nice lot, which was awarded to her in the divorce, and dreamed about building on that spot. It was a beautiful piece of land in an older neighborhood, surrounded by fifteen palm trees. The trees were situated in such a way that they wouldn't have to be cut down to make way for a three-bedroom house. She'd had an architect draw plans for the house and knew the costs. To do it, she would need to sell her house here, but she was dragging her feet.

As we were walking into the mall, I threw out, "Did I mention to you that we're going to try to do a little focus study with the Mall Walking Club about Friendly Neighbors? Kent seemed interested in helping."

"I guess I overheard something about that. I think it'll be interesting to try and get some answers from these geezers. A lot of the time most of them look pretty vacant," she whispered.

"Wow—that's kind of harsh, Mom. These are *your* people."

I saw Kent talking to one of the mall managers who often walks around in the mornings with a clipboard. You could tell he was always pondering how to fill the recently vacated retail spaces. Kent waved me over. "Hi, Julie. You've met Henry before." Henry nodded. "He's offered us the use of an empty kiosk over by the food court as a home base for our focus study."

"That's great. Thanks so much. We shouldn't need it for more than three days, and probably just from 8 to 10 in the morning."

"Fine by me, just leave it as you found it when you're done."

He walked off and Kent and I started discussing the approach. I had already crafted a questionnaire that would give us the basic information we needed. It included asking them if they use a smartphone, live in their own home, utilize help in the home, any problems they encounter, and a few other questions. I kept it short and sweet, so we didn't lose their attention. The plan was to fine-tune it that night and start the project the next day. Mom was standing by, and I could tell she was getting annoyed. The app idea was of no interest to her, and she hated technology. I was constantly fixing some strange occurrence on her laptop so she could continue her search for the best way to keep wisteria vines blooming or learn how to make a peach pie with even more calories. When she got annoyed, she had this way of looking right at me while I talked to someone else, so I could feel her eyes burning into my soul. So, we wrapped it up and finished the walk with Kent.

We arrived early the next day to do the setup. I had shortened the questionnaire to only eight questions. We also decided to offer cookies as an incentive. It seemed a little counterproductive since people were walking for their health, but celery never seems to lure people in. The plan was for Kent and Suzanne to bring people over so I could hit them quickly with the questionnaire. Seemed simple enough.

The first person to stop by was Kent's pal, Frank.

"Hi, Frank. Thanks so much for taking the time to help with this project. I only have eight questions and then you can be on your way with a delicious chocolate chip cookie."

"Jule, I don't eat cookies anymore since my doctor is a fascist and forbids sugar, but I want to help anyway."

"OK, Question 1. What is your age?"

"72."

"Question 2. Do you use a smartphone?"

"Well, I'll tell you. It's the damn cell phones that are ruining society. Everyone is so distracted that they are forgetting things like, 'Hey, did I feed my family?' Or better yet, 'Did I leave my baby in the car?' How does someone forget that they left their kid in the car? That's a real asshole right there. Yeah, you see the idiots even walking through here staring at their phones. We should put more deadly obstacles in hallways and on sidewalks so that if they don't pay attention, they could fall into a pit or something. That would get people to start looking up."

I had to stop him, or this could go on for a while. "So, I am assuming that's a 'no' to smartphone use," as I started to note the answer.

"No, Jule, it's a yes. I *do* use a smartphone. Most days it annoys me, but I use it. You must have one, or you'll be left behind. But I hate them!"

"OK, Frank, let's move on, then."

It went on like this for most of the volunteers I questioned. There were lots of explanations to go along with the answers, and I'd thought the questions were straightforward. How do you turn a question like, "Do you live in your own home?" into a ten-minute explanation? The answers included a lot of personal information, extras about their worthless kids, and health problems that were TMI and unrelated; although, I have to say that it was fun and very insightful. After three days, I had a good amount of data. Even though it was a small sample size, it was the perfect demographic. From here, I could create the proposal outline and move forward. The next step would be to build and test the financial model. I also needed to find someone to craft a wireframe of the application screen by screen from the outline. Based on this experience, the main goal would be to keep the final product super simple.

This was going to be a long haul, but I was getting excited about the possibility of a worthwhile project.

Chapter 9
The Holiday

HI, MY NAME IS JULIE, and I am a Christmas-aholic. I have tried to get help for my addiction, but it just grows brighter and more out of control every year. I start getting ramped up and overly excited right after Halloween even though I don't act on it until the day after Thanksgiving. (I'm not a monster, after all!) You absolutely must give Thanksgiving its day since it is probably the least selfish of all the holidays. It's just loving family and friends, having a great meal, and getting together to be thankful. You can't crowd Thanksgiving. But, as soon as that last bit of turkey is gobbled up, it's over—Christmas is on! I will decorate anything that will hold a colorful swag, vintage ornament, or a string of white lights.

I have a special room designated just for Christmas storage. In there are stacks of boxes overflowing with decorations organized by room and tree number. I have a total of six, yes s-i-x, trees that I display in assigned rooms in my home.

The addiction extends into other areas as well, like my secret fantasy of having a chocolate martini, adorned with peppermint sticks while Santa and I chill in a picturesque holiday-themed bar up north. For some reason, I never mention that fantasy to Mark. Or the issue of spending an excessive amount of time "pinning" Christmas ideas year-round when I should be focused on something else. Or the dedication to watching my all-time favorite Christmas movies and the Hallmark channel lineup that pits a romance against miscommunication, interrupted kisses, and meddling townsfolk. Somehow, against all odds, love always wins in the end. My family has come to accept my sick addiction and knows that I will always host Christmas Day, so they don't even try to suggest any other plan. It would not be pretty to mess with me at this time of year.

This Christmas would be a first. I had decided to have the entire family for the holiday. That included my father (no dumbass dates allowed), my three siblings and their families, and of course, Mom and Kylie. Dad and Mom had not been together to celebrate anything since their divorce many years earlier. I was nervous as it was a little like putting out a fire with gasoline, but I thought, what the hell, let's see how it goes.

I picked up Kylie at the airport two days before Christmas. She planned to stay for six days. During these days, she would also see her father, and we had worked out a schedule. She would be with him for Christmas Eve and then come over to our house for Christmas dinner and the day after (which is my birthday). The other days would be flexible, depending on what she had planned. There were also childhood friends for her to see, so there was a lot on her plate. I tried not to make it too demanding because she has melted down in the past with a jam-packed family schedule.

I finally saw her when she came down the ramp into the baggage area. "Oh my God, I cannot and will not stop hugging you! I am so excited to see you, Kylie!" The tight squeeze was more than just an embrace, it was the culmination of realizing that my little girl was an adult. She was now coming and going into my life on her timeline. It hit me that I now needed her maybe more than she needed me.

"I know, this is perfect. I'm so glad to be home. You have no idea how bad I needed this trip. Where's Grandma, didn't she come with you?"

"Oh, she was still in bed, so I told her I'd grab you and call her immediately after."

"Mom, that's weird. She decided to sleep instead of coming to get me?"

"Don't read anything into it. It's 8:00 a.m. and you know she probably didn't even fall asleep until 3!"

"Oh, right. I forget that the night owl can't go to bed at any normal time. I can't wait to see her, too."

We grabbed her super large suitcase that had been labeled "heavy" by the airport staff and headed to the doors. I'm sure an airport employee already used a few choice words when they had to load it on the conveyor. I didn't bother to ask what was in it because I already knew. Christmas presents for everyone. Boho chic outfits for any occasion and hair and makeup items that would rival any salon's collection.

"So, Mom, last time we talked, you said something insane. You said that Grandpa is coming over for Christmas dinner. Were you high on Christmas or just plain drunk?"

"I'll admit I could have been buzzing when I came up with the idea, but Suzanne is OK with it, and it seems like the right time to give it a try. I told them both: best behavior and no significant others."

"Yeah, sure, what could possibly go wrong here, Mom?" We both laughed as I pulled a groin muscle trying to hoist that damn bag into my SUV.

Since she brought it up, the dinner was starting to worry me a little, but it was Christmas and nothing bad happens at Christmas—at least not according to Hallmark.

On the 24th, my mom and Kylie came over for breakfast so we could have a little alone time. We had great fun sipping mimosas and eating cinnamon rolls and bacon.

"Gram, what the hell have you been doing? I can tell that you've really lost some weight! How much is it?"

"I'm sure your mom told you I had slimmed down a little bit. I think it's about twenty-five pounds altogether. I'm eating less and have been walking at the mall and getting a little aerobic workout in from time to time with a man friend." She whispered the last part as she pantomimed a thrusting motion. We all laughed.

"Yes! Get it, Grandma! I've heard about this man friend, and I'm happy for you. Are you having a good time?"

"At this age, I'm simply happy that someone finds me attractive, Kylie. He's fun to be around, and we like each other."

"Kent is great, and I really like him," I added with a full mouth. The cinnamon rolls were exceptional, and I was carb-loading for the holidays as usual.

"Are we going to meet him tomorrow, Gram?"

"No, your Drill Sergeant Mom has forbidden any SOs. That means 'significant others,' but you probably already knew that, Kylie."

"Is that what it means? Yup, it's a good rule with Grandpa coming this year. Are you OK with this?" Kylie asked, trying to keep the question light.

"I don't give a flying fart what he does, and it will save all of you from having two separate Christmas parties if we are all together. As long as he doesn't try to lure me under the mistletoe, I'm good. My plan is to stay away from him."

Well, we knew instantly that was total BS. She would find an opportunity to jab him somehow. She claimed she didn't care, but she was still trying to administer revenge for the cheating humiliation she experienced years ago. I'm sure she thought he hadn't suffered enough. She just wouldn't be able to help herself!

Christmas morning began quiet and magically beautiful. The trees had a shimmering coat of snow. We lived on a two-acre wooded lot up on a hill surrounded by trees. Our house was in a gated neighborhood and was way too large for the two of us, at seven thousand square feet. However, when we hosted a holiday, it worked out perfectly. With five guest rooms, we could keep anyone who wanted to stay overnight. We fell in love with the neighborhood, which looked like it could be anywhere in northern Michigan, with tall lodge pine trees and mature oaks. It was a gorgeous backdrop to the perfect white Christmas.

I was already in a great mood and Mark and I were happy to be alone before the partygoers arrived with their holiday hang-ups. We had coffee and exchanged our own gifts while we listened to Christmas music. My family was due at 2:00 p.m. It was the calm before the yuletide storm. Maybe this time it would be like a sappy Christmas movie. A girl can dream, or better yet, pray.

The first to arrive for any family function was always my brother, Jeff, and his wife, YuMei. Shortly after Jeff's arrival was my sister, Jenny, and her family. She had four kids and they were all there, even the oldest, Grayson, who was home from college. Then there were her three girls, Erin, Avery, and Eve and her hand-some husband, Bob. A little later was my younger brother, Jon, and his girlfriend, Hannah; they picked up my mom on their way over. He also had his two kids with him, Max and Veronica, who were in college as well. Kylie arrived, and everyone wanted to catch up with her since she hadn't been home in quite a while. As the family was happily chatting and getting drinks in the kitchen, my dad arrived at the front door.

"Hi, Jule. Merry Christmas. It looks beautiful up here, so fes-tive," he said as he looked around from the foyer.

"You know me, Dad. Never met a Christmas decoration that I didn't like, even the tacky ones!"

"I have some gifts here. I'll put them under this tree—is that where they go?" He pointed to a red and gold decorated tree in the tall foyer. "Also, where is the Christmas Witch?"

"No, Dad, we'll do gifts in the living room, around the corner. There's a tree in there for the family gifts. Also, please don't start that crap. But she's in the kitchen."

He winked and headed off to the tree, and I went to the kitchen to check on dinner.

"Mom, he's here. He seems to be in a particularly good mood, so hopefully, all is well," I said while moving things around on the counter to make more room.

"Like I said, Julie, I don't give a rat's ass what he does. It's Christmas, and we will have a good day." Her sense of calm did not make me feel better.

The greetings were appropriate and uneventful. It was like waiting for a shoe to drop or a bomb to detonate, but we all tried to act cool. Dinner was filet mignon and lobster with all the decadent side dishes. Mark was a fantastic cook, and my family loved his creations.

Hannah had on a cute red fit-and-flare dress and a Santa hat, so she was nominated to play Santa. Her assignment was to get the gifts from under the tree and my little nieces would then take them to the recipient. This seemed harmless enough until about four gifts in. Mom put down her third peppermint martini and said, "Am I the only one who has noticed that your sick father is looking down this sweet woman's dress every time she grabs a gift from under the tree? She does look a little inappropriate, like a sexy elf, but come on, really? Even the birthday of innocent baby Jesus is not off-limits to your depravity!" Mom exclaimed, and then took a demure swig of her flavored cocktail and steadied herself with her free hand.

There was a stunned hush over the group. We weren't sure we'd heard her correctly and even if we did, what the hell do you do? My dad was looking blankly at her, sort of like someone who had been caught in the act.

"Now, Mom, I'm sure you're mistaken. Not very nice, either. This might be time to slow down on the martinis," Jon said, quietly giving me the side-eye. He was clearly sending me a signal to do something, so I acted.

"Yeah, Mom, why don't you come into the kitchen and help me with dessert?"

"Whatever, Jule. Just pointing out the obvious. A leopard can't change its spots. He just *has* to look. I'll come with you, but don't yell at me for pointing out what everyone saw."

Kylie followed as well, and we got into the kitchen where I

took the martini out of Mom's hand. "Maybe give this a rest for a minute. You were doing so well, but that was ridiculously awkward. You know the grandkids are in the room, right? Poor Hannah probably feels super weird as well. Welcome to our Christmas, Hannah! What are you thinking?"

"Grandma, that was insane but funny as hell," Kylie giggled.

"Ky, if you're going to be here, please try to help," I gritted through my teeth as I gave her a stern look.

"Just stating the obvious. You saw it, right? He just can't help himself," Mom said flatly.

"OK, Mom, do you need a little time to chill? We have a lot of holiday left here. I have all your stuff in the downstairs guest bedroom. Maybe a few minutes to lie down and regroup?"

"Julie, whatever. I just said what other people were thinking. I'll go down there mostly because I am nicely buzzed, but I don't want to miss the rest of the day, so please come and get me in a little bit."

Kylie grabbed my shoulder once Mom went down the stairs. "Still think this was a great idea, Mom?"

"Not so much right now."

We went back into the living room and everything was back on track. As usual, everyone was acting like nothing had happened and trying to salvage the day. When we finished the gifts and cleaned up the paper, people resumed chatting and milling around the house. The smaller children played with their new gadgets and the day seemed restored to normal. My brothers were teasing Dad about the golf accessories he had given them. "It's going to take more than these to improve Jon's game!" Jeff joked. I took the opportunity to head downstairs and check on Mom.

When I stepped into the guest room, the bed was empty, and the covers were not moved. I walked around to the side opposite the door and there she was, slumped on the floor. I immediately called her name, but she did not respond. I knelt and turned her on her side. Her eyes fluttered open and she started to sit up.

"Oh my God, Mom! Are you OK?"

She said something nonsensical and continued to blink her eyes. After a few seconds, she said, "What happened?"

"I don't know, I came in and you were on the floor. Are you hurt at all?"

"No, just feel kinda groggy and don't remember how I got down on the floor. Help me up."

I lifted her to the side of the bed, and she seemed wide awake now.

"You doing OK? Did you faint?"

"I really don't remember. Just give me a minute and I'll be fine. By the way, is the leopard still here?"

"Yup, he's still here, and the family seems to have gotten past the bomb you dropped earlier."

"Well, that was absolutely a fact and I stand by what I said," she muttered while getting her bearings.

I went into the bathroom and got a cool washcloth. Her color was normal, and she was starting to act like nothing had happened. I kept her talking as I put the cold compress on her forehead. We sat for a while and then she insisted on rejoining the group. We headed upstairs and had a great time playing cards and games for the rest of the night. She switched to an unspiked punch and we kept her away from my father. He behaved like a choir boy, so no more drama on that front. Mark and I even managed to pull off a festive family photo in front of the foyer Christmas tree with all the grandkids on the circular staircase. I planned to get copies to everyone since this was unprecedented.

When the night wound down, I couldn't shake the incident with Mom. I thought at first that maybe it was the martinis, but that didn't make sense. She had been a little buzzed from the drinks and didn't eat much at dinner but seemed fine. I mean, the outburst was crazy, but par behavior even for sober Suzanne. I made a note to call Dr. Manning again and push some tests after the holiday. I was not going to accept the lackadaisical attitude of that oversexed cougar.

Chapter 10
The Fifties

OH NO, the day after Christmas and my fiftieth birthday. Not a red-letter day for me, but everyone else wanted to continue the party. We had most of the family sleepover, and like mice in a cheese maze hunt, they started emerging from various parts of the house to have coffee, breakfast casserole, and muffins while they nursed hangovers. My dad had gone home, which was for the best. I couldn't blame him after being publicly shamed. I still to this day do not know if he was looking down Hannah's dress, but it isn't unbelievable given his history. When you have a track record of being a horny old dude, you don't get the benefit of the doubt in these situations.

As the day progressed, I started to get suspicious about a surprise birthday party. I had made it very clear that I only wanted a family dinner and nothing more. It was soon obvious that no one listened to me as a catering van pulled up to deliver trays of delectable appetizers and diet-busting desserts.

"OK, Mark, what is going on here?" I asked suspiciously. "I told you no party!"

"Julie, everyone has been asking me what's happening for your birthday, so I just started inviting people over. It's going to be cocktails, appetizers, and desserts. I'm trying to keep it simple, but you must feed people. You can't just pump them full of liquor and send them on their way."

"Oh my gosh, you sneaky bastard—who did you invite?" I was not amused.

"Well, your family, the neighbor friends, the marina peeps, and most of your gal pals and their husbands."

"So, a small gathering of fifty people? You are in deep trouble."

"You know you'll have fun if you just give it a chance. Go get dressed, people are arriving in about an hour. Also, you don't scare me."

Mark flashed me the smile that gets him anything he wants, and I turned to Mom and Kylie. "You guys are involved in this, too, aren't you?"

"Julie, you never want any attention, and it's about time we get back at you for all the unwanted bullshit parties you've thrown for us over the years," Mom said.

"OK, OK. I'll suck it up and have a good time. Thanks, guys, this is a nice-ish idea." I headed toward my room while giving them double middle fingers. They laughed and returned the gesture.

Despite my misgivings, the party was fabulous, and I was happy to see so many of our friends. There were even old workmates from the newspaper who I hadn't seen in quite a few months. They had all left after the merger, and it was nice to catch up. Halfway through the night, one of my closest friends, Tammy, came up and bumped my arm.

"Hey, Julie, can I steal you away for a minute?" We headed back to the master suite and she shut the door. I started to get a little worried because I had known Tammy for more than twenty years and she'd never acted this seriously. Most of the time we were mocking others and laughing until we peed a little.

"What's up, Tams? Is something wrong?"

"Oh, not really, but I'm kind of concerned. I hadn't seen your mom in a few months, and she looks really thin to me. I complimented her, and she said something strange. She said, 'That's what happens, Tam, when you can't swallow food anymore.' I said, 'What do you mean, Suz?' because you know your mom throws out some crazy shit every now and then. She said, 'Well, sometimes it's really hard for me to swallow.' Then Jeff came up and we started talking about something else. What's going on, Jules?"

"Wow, I don't really know. I've never heard her say that before. I eat with her about three to four times a week, and she really doesn't eat much these days, but I thought she was just working on her fitness. She never mentioned anything about swallowing. I went to her doctor's appointment with her about three months ago and everything seemed fine. I've been a little more worried lately after I found her semi-passed out in a guest room yesterday, but she had been drinking. Oh God, now I'm really concerned."

"That does seem a little scary. I didn't want to drop this to you at your party, but it was weird, and I didn't want to forget to tell you. You know how it goes with this bullshit menopause memory."

"Oh, I know, me too, and I'm glad that you told me. I'm going to call her doctor tomorrow and see if we can get in this week. I'll keep you posted. Did I ever tell you about this horny doctor she has?"

I filled her in on Dr. Manning's sexual exploits as we returned to the party, and we had a good laugh. But I was thinking about the swallowing comment. My mom had a history of keeping things from people who then found out when she couldn't keep it quiet anymore. This was something that would keep me awake tonight. Was it a throat tumor? Or worse, brain cancer? Or was she just trying to get a rise out of Tammy? I looked over, and she was having a great time laughing with our neighbors and seemed perfectly fine. Clearly, we needed to talk.

Later in the evening, I had a chance to hang out with Kylie when people started heading out the door. I had spent the least amount of time with her: Christmas had been busy and the birthday party was hectic as well. She was questioning me about the

Friendly Neighbors mobile app. She knew that I was pursuing something but had no details. A few of my friends had mentioned it to her at the party, which piqued her interest. I filled her in, but she was nervous about the process.

"Mom, I think it's a great idea, but this could end up taking a lot of money to get off the ground."

"Yes, I know, and I'm pretty sure that Mark is not on board to finance the process. I think he's basically putting up with my crazy idea until it runs its course and I go back to corporate America."

"Don't go back if you can avoid it, Mom. Corporations suck and I've only been in the work world for a couple of years. So many dicks who don't do much of anything while the rest of us hard-charging drones do all the grunt work and make way less money. I'd get out if I could, but at my age, I need to pay my dues to the corporate gods," she said through a mouth stuffed with cake. The house was quiet now, and we were using our hands to pick at birthday leftovers.

Even though she questioned corporate structure, Kylie was doing well in Denver. She was working for a digital marketing firm and had been promoted twice already.

"You know, Mom, you should try to find some financing as soon as the idea is viable."

"I have a guy working on the layout and an overall concept for the wireframe based on my notes and research. He told me that he would have something for me to look at next week. He's sweet but kind of a strange ranger, as most developers are. I can hear Adult Swim cartoons in the background when we talk, but mostly, he just wants to text me progress. He's always suggesting some new way to communicate, like using WhatsApp. I never know what the hell he's talking about; he uses a lot of tech acronyms. I mean, I'm good to text, but that's as far as it goes. I found him through a friend of a friend, so I don't have much firsthand knowledge of his abilities. He came highly recommended as someone who produces great work. When that's ready, I plan to shop it at IdeaLab in Detroit."

"Great idea, Mom. I heard they have a lot of private investment money waiting for new technology businesses."

"It may be just what I need to get things off the ground. Or there will be zero interest, and it will fall flat. Just gotta go balls-out, right? I may need your help when I get to the digital marketing options if we even get that far."

"Now come on, Mom, you always told me that confidence is half the battle. Don't make a liar out of yourself!"

I gave her a hug and we talked about the next time we would see each other. She had a few more days in town, but they would be spent with her father. It was always a rough goodbye. I loved her so much as a daughter, but she had also become a wonderful friend.

That holiday week, I called Dr. Manning's office and left a message on the nurse's line to get an appointment for my mom. Tracy called me back but said only my mom could request an appointment because of HIPAA laws. I called Mom and told her that I was stopping by on my way to the store. This could be a conversation where she blew off the idea of going back to the doctor, but I was going to insist. When I arrived at her house, Winnie the spaz was jumping on me at the door. As usual, Winnie practically molested me as I maneuvered past. That dog really needed more obedience classes, or maybe a long-term boarding school. I gave her the obligatory attention to keep her from ripping my cashmere sweater and then proceeded into the living room. Mom was sitting in one of the club chairs with all sorts of magazines and bills spread out in front of her. She had made some uneven piles, but it looked like organized chaos.

"Hi, Mom. How are you after this crazy week?"

"Hi, Jule. I'm feeling a little tired but trying to clean up some of this stuff that I've let pile up."

I really wanted to keep this conversation light and easy so that she would speak to me with some honesty. I knew if I came at this the wrong way, I would get nowhere with her.

"Do you need some help?" I bent to pick up one of the piles of gardening catalogs and magazines.

"Sure, you can throw that pile into the garbage bag right there. I've read all of those many times and don't need to order any more solar globe lights or exotic tulip bulbs, although they are pretty."

The other piles were old bills that she had paid but kept around with various notes on them. She always had an insecurity about bills and money that stemmed from growing up poor. She had some telling habits, like saving tin foil. The cabinets were full of Ziploc bags. She would wash them after use and hang them over her dish rack to dry. These items would only get tossed if they had holes or large tears, or if my sister or I cleaned the kitchen and threw things away. Even then, it was always a struggle. We had to push them to the bottom of the trash bin, so she didn't notice. Her financial insecurities were deeply rooted and further galvanized by the divorce when the alimony stopped coming after many years.

There was another pile of photographs and an old sketchbook from her father that she must have dug out of a storage box. Her dad rode to work in a carpool with some of the neighbors, and one day, there was an accident. It was a very traumatic time in her family. The sketchbook was full of drawings he had done as a hobby when he was little. Now they must have been very comforting to her. I had leafed through them numerous times over the years. Most of the sketches were in pencil, but he'd used colored pencils, too. They were primarily nature drawings like trees, and close-ups of leaves. He had also drawn things in school when he was bored. There were cartoon characters and landscape scenes from outside the classroom windows. He had had real talent, but it was never pursued any further. I know the sketchbook meant a lot to her, and after her mother died, she somehow snagged it without any of her other siblings knowing about it.

I eased into the conversation with caution. "Did you have a good time this week? Wasn't it great to see everyone?"

"I did have a good time considering that your dad was there, and I lost it a little bit. But all in all, I had fun. I did notice that I was more tired than usual, and it's been happening more often lately. Of course, the holidays are always stressful."

This was going to be easier than I thought since she had opened the door for me. If the conversation were initiated by her, it would go a lot better.

"So, Mom, I wanted to ask you about something, and I really need you to be honest with me. Are you having a problem with eating and swallowing?"

"Dammit, Julie, I knew I shouldn't have said anything to Tams. She always runs right to you. I love her, but what a mouth."

"Mom, this isn't on Tammy. Are you having some issues that I need to know about?"

There was a long pause. "OK, sometimes it does feel like there's something in my throat that makes it hard to swallow. That is why I eat less and chew very slowly. Some days it isn't as bad, but lots of times, I really notice it."

"I think that's a good reason to head back to Dr. Manning and see if there are some tests that need to be taken. What do you think?" I looked over as her eyes welled up with tears as she nodded her head. I got up and hugged her, and then she went into a full-on cry.

"I probably have throat cancer. I'm in real trouble."

"Oh, Mom, don't jump to conclusions—we'll get it figured out. Things are always worse in your head when you think about all the terrible scenarios and then you find out it's not a big deal. Remember when I had that horrible rash and convinced myself that it was the first phase of Ebola? Eventually, I found out it was an allergic reaction to that skincare line made from old citrus fruit that was supposed to make me look ten years younger. So, let's start trying to find out what's going on, and then you can stop worrying about all the horrible possibilities."

Like many moms, she was a professional "worrier" from way

back and had been perfecting the skill since she was a child. I was more worried than I let on, but I hoped she'd bought it. She probably saw right through me, but it was a step in the right direction.

Chapter 11
The ENT

AFTER MOM'S SECOND ATTEMPT to set up an appointment, I was ready to go off on our friend Nurse Tracy. It seemed that they were super backed up after the holidays and she didn't have anything open until the third week in January. Dr. Manning had also just returned from a vacation in Hawaii (no doubt a bangfest), and that wasn't making things any easier. I told Mom to give me the phone.

"Hi, Tracy, this is Julie, her daughter. I am not sure if she explained this to you clearly enough, so I'm going to go through it with you again. My mother really needs to get in there as I'm sure that she will need a referral for some other tests. Her swallowing is delayed sometimes and has caused her to actually choke. It is not normal, and I am very concerned."

I glanced over to reassure Mom since I didn't want her to get upset at my exaggerated urgency. She was staring straight at me and even nodded her head a little in agreement, which was a good sign.

"I understand," Nurse Tracy said. "Let me talk to the doctor and see if we can bump another patient or open up a slot somewhere. I'll call you right back."

I hung up and turned to Mom. "She better fucking call back soon or I'll make an extremely awkward in-person appearance, or better yet, sick this crazed doodle on her ass!" For emphasis, I threw Winnie's ball and she went bounding down the hall after it.

"Dr. Manning does seem to be a little checked out these days. I think she's focused mostly on dick and retirement," Mom responded with a smirk. "In that order."

"Unfortunately, I can't help her with either of those, but if Dr. Humpy doesn't get her act together soon, I might spread the word on social media that she has a raging STD." We both laughed.

We wound up with an appointment for the next day, first thing in the morning.

Tracy had Mom step on the scale before we went into the exam room and said, "Wow, Suzanne, you're down another twenty pounds. That's thirty-five pounds altogether since last year."

I gave her a sharp look and turned to my mom. "Did you know you had lost that much weight?"

"Well, I haven't checked it lately, but I did need to get some smaller jeans. You know I have a new boyfriend, and I'm trying to keep myself hot. Anyway, you can never be too thin, right?"

She had been gulping a little bit at dinner last night. How long had I been missing the signs that there was something wrong? Why did it seem so clear now, and why would she have hidden this from me?

Dr. Manning breezed into the room. She had a slight tan, newly acquired hair extensions, and too much perfume. I guess her trip had been a success in more ways than one. "Hi, Suzanne. Tracy mentioned that we needed to see you about a swallowing issue. Please fill me in on what's been going on. I need all the details." I guess it was right down to business since we had been wedged into an appointment slot. No pleasantries today, thank God.

"Hi, Dr. Manning. Well, I've been noticing some weird sensations in my throat that cause me to hesitate when I swallow. I seem to chew for a long time before I feel like it's OK to try to swallow. I don't necessarily choke, but I do feel like I am *going* to choke sometimes," Mom explained carefully.

The doctor had already moved closer to her and was listening intently while she studied the chart. "Hmmm, that may explain the weight loss. How long has this been going on?"

Mom looked over at me and then said, "Probably three or four months."

"Oh my God, Mom, you started feeling this last fall and didn't say anything? Are you sure?"

Nurse Tracy and the good doctor seemed surprised at my reaction. They didn't know that I talked to this woman every single day. How could she not mention this?

"Yes, Julie. I first noticed it around my birthday but thought it was no big deal, maybe some acid reflux or whatever. Then it kept happening, and I started to think that I should tell you, but it was Christmas, then your birthday ..." Her voice trailed off and I found myself staring out the window at a big pile of snow that the parking lot plows had pushed to one side. The blinds were pulled halfway down, but I could still get a sense of the height. It was amazing how tall and dirty some of those piles could get before the temperature rose enough to melt them into a slushy mess.

I was feeling frustrated and annoyed when I turned back to Mom as she sat quietly. My frustration was partially with her lack of information and partially with myself for not seeing this in the first place. I was also sympathetic at the same time because this seemed like a turning point of some sort, but what was next?

Dr. Manning looked in Mom's throat with a penlight while the room was noticeably quiet. After a few minutes, I realized that I was holding my breath. As I exhaled, she said, "I don't see any blockage myself; it all looks fine from here. But let's refer you on to an ENT to get a closer look." Then she used her otoscope to check the ears. "Yes, I'd like you to see Dr. Folberg. He's a good Ear Nose and Throat guy over in the Meritas complex. He'll do a laryngoscopy right in his office to get a better view. Tracy, can you call and set that up for Suzanne?"

Tracy nodded and stepped out of the room. Dr. Manning pushed her stool back and said, "What else can I help you with?"

Mom looked over at me and then slowly spoke. "I think that my antidepressant has stopped working. I'm really feeling down lately and have been waking up a lot, and then I'm not able to get back to sleep."

This was another bit of news that Mom had not shared with me. My mom had been on antidepressants ever since I could remember. She was mostly an incredibly fun and upbeat person, but there was a dark side, and I've known about it since I was a child. She was in a "facility" while pregnant with me. She was let out at Christmas time and that's when I was born, on the 26th. When she was pregnant with me, she thought hormones were causing her mood swings—the baby blues from having my older brother—but my dad described it a little more seriously than that. She was having trouble coping and couldn't take proper care of my brother, Jeff, who was two years old. My dad would come home from work and Mom would be locked in the bedroom while Jeff cried in his playpen in the living room. Dad was just starting his career with General Motors and was overwhelmed with trying to manage the situation at home. His mother, my grandmother, stayed for a few months until things leveled out, but they never completely disappeared.

There weren't many options for mental health care in the 1960s, so eventually, Mom took a "rest" at a place called Oakwood that was staffed by nuns. At that time, tranquilizers were the usual path, and that evolved into other medications. She had been prescribed all of them at one time or another. On multiple occasions, she and I talked about this time in her life over a few glasses of wine. I could only imagine the sadness and despair she had experienced as she struggled with the illness. She was incredibly open about it and detailed the therapies and treatments she had been through over the years—even a few shock therapy sessions. She had anger about this time in her life and the ignorance that surrounded mental illness and the often-barbaric treatments that were used. Some things worked for a while, but the results never lasted. She also saw a therapist here and there and was eventually correctly diagnosed with depression. A chemical reaction in her body caused her to feel sadness and despair; it wasn't within her control.

She gave me that look of hers, and I knew she felt bad that her chronic depression was possibly now compromising her physical health.

"I can give you an additional pill that will help the effectiveness of your Amitriptyline. I want you to get more rest at night." She wrote out a prescription form (still refusing to use the laptop) and handed it to me.

I smiled at Mom because I knew she was measuring my reaction. She was always trying to make up for her depression issues. I knew she still felt we were short changed as kids with the "mental mom." None of us have ever felt that way, but it still bothered her.

We got back into the car and she said, "Well, I guess I should feel a little relieved that she didn't see a big, fat, oozing tumor."

I laughed, "Yup, that's a good sign. Nurse Tracy told me on the way out that she was able to get you into Dr. Folberg, the ENT guy, on Monday at 10. I'll find out where it is and pick you up."

"Julie, I'm sure you have other things to do. I can get there."

"This is an actual test, Mom. They may even give you some sort of anesthesia. Of course, I am going with you. I want to find out what's going on just as much as you do. We know it's not a big, fat, oozing tumor, so let's see what Folberg thinks." I kept it light and breezy, but I was just as concerned as she was about this test.

Dr. Leo Folberg was what I'd call a distinguished-looking man. He had sandy-colored hair mixed with some gray and a handsome face with a square jawline. He wore a white doctor's coat, with his name stitched over the left side in navy-blue italic letters. His shoes were black suede Gucci loafers. His clothes under the coat were impeccable. Most likely Tom Ford, light blue shirt with French cuffs, and round gold cufflinks. The slacks had small gray pinstripes with a designer cut. I couldn't get a good look at the watch, but it was gorgeous, heavy, probably a Rolex or TAG Heuer. The ENT business must be very, very good.

He made us feel at ease right away with great eye contact and charming small talk. He really listened to my mom, which was sometimes a rare quality in a doctor. I could see why he was at the top of the referral list.

"Suzanne, it sounds like this sensation of choking has been going on for a good amount of time. Three months, is that correct?"

"Yes, I didn't give it much attention until a few weeks ago when I really felt the choking sensation while eating at home alone."

Oh, so now I get it. The sympathy card was the game we were going to play with Dr. Hotness. Eating at home ALONE. Nice, but I had already noticed the classy gold band. I'm sure she had, too, but just couldn't help herself. He didn't bite and kept it purely professional, which was a nice change from Dr. Humpy.

"Since this has been going on for a few months, I want to do a direct laryngoscopy. This will involve a fiber optic laryngoscope. It's a very flexible cable that fits easily through your nostril and down your throat."

"That sounds awful, doctor," Mom said, quickly shooting me a look.

"We'll alleviate any discomfort with some numbing spray. It'll be over quickly, but I want to have a good look and this small telescope will provide that for us. I assure you it sounds worse than it is." He flashed a smile. That worked; Mom would have let the guy perform a spinal tap at that point.

As promised, the procedure was short and painless. She gagged just a little when he put the small cable down, but that was all. After he pulled the scope out, he looked directly at Mom and said he saw nothing to be concerned about. There were no growths or masses in her throat or nose. He explained that she could use ice chips or gargle if her throat was sore from the procedure, but that it should feel fine.

"So, what could be causing her choking sensation?" I asked. I was relieved, but nothing was resolved. We were still at square one.

"There are several things that could be a potential cause, but none of them are directly related to the functioning of her throat. My recommendation is to go back to Dr. Manning and explore additional tests, like a CT scan or MRI." And with that vague follow-up, he tapped her leg, smiled, and he and his nameless nurse (who cared about her?) went out the door.

"Well, good news about the throat, right, Mom?"

"Yeah, but why do I still feel something going on? Do you think I could be imagining this? Maybe it's psychosomatic?"

"No, probably just psycho. I'm kidding! We'll push this further until we get an answer. In the meantime, we have a chance to get more kinky stories from Dr. Hornball."

Mom looked at me, smiled, and nodded while she got down from the exam chair. I could feel her sense of relief. We wrapped it up at the desk and headed home.

On the drive back, I kept thinking about the time she was my Homeroom Mother, planning holiday class parties, and getting other parents involved. She would arrive—to the excitement of my class—with chocolate cupcakes, games, decorations, and my toddler sister in tow. Or when she was the Girl Scout leader of my twelve-member troop in fourth grade. Even though she had four kids and many responsibilities at home, she made time to take the troop camping (which we knew she hated), to craft classes, and swim safety lessons, and helped us all earn numerous badges. She had been there so many times, and I was glad I could help her through this uncertain time as well.

Back at Dr. Manning's office, her next idea was twofold: Get my mom to a neurologist and do an MRI of her head and throat. The test was scheduled but wouldn't take place for a few weeks. We were still searching for a neurologist who was accepting new patients in our area.

Mom was more tired and not interested in walking in the mornings anymore. Most of that was because of her depression and concern about her health. Kent and Lorri had made a habit of stopping over once or twice a week to take her out. We also had her at our house quite a bit for dinner and movies. She was feeling down, and each day, the uncertainty was taking a lot out of her. I looked for ways to keep her spirits up and had one idea that Kylie and I were working on, which was a surprise visit.

Chapter 12
The Surprises

OLIVER, the wireframe developer for Friendly Neighbors, called to set up a meeting. Up to this point, we had talked on the phone and via email but had never met in person. He wanted me to come to his place, so he could show me the layout on his computer. This way we could make any changes on the fly and wrap it up quickly. He lived in an upper-level apartment in an old house near the downtown area. I showed up on a snowy afternoon in early February. Days like this, I was glad I drove an SUV that could handle the slippery and unpredictable Michigan roads. I had to park on the street because the driveway was already full of three battered cars. I got out and looked up to a two-story brick house with a long front porch and stone columns. The house was rundown; it had probably seen its prime around 1940. I started to worry a little bit about my choices. Was I entrusting the successful creation of my business to an agoraphobic millennial?

Oliver was recommended by a contact from my previous life in media. He had worked in a software development firm creating apps for a few years right out of college. For some reason, he had gone out on his own and now worked out of this house. The outside didn't look very well maintained, and I hoped that wasn't an indication of his level of success. I rang the doorbell for apartment 2B and heard him clomp down the stairs. There was a dog bark from the lower apartment and a yell for the dog to shut up. Oliver opened the door, and the first impression was exactly what I had pictured from our phone conversations. He was average height, shoulder-length brown hair, slightly wavy, hazel eyes, and a very slim build. He was either smiling or grimacing, but it was hard to tell which. Maybe that was because of screen overexposure and limited interaction with people in the real world. He opened the door wide to welcome me.

"Hi, Julie, so nice to finally meet you in person. Hope you didn't have a rough trip over here today. The snow just never seems to let up."

"I know! It's great to meet you as well. The trip over was pretty typical for our Michigan February. I'm excited to see what you've come up with for Friendly Neighbors." I entered the small entry area and we started up the stairway.

The apartment was nicely done and had an open floor plan for an older building. There had been some renovations in recent years and Oliver had a good aesthetic. The furniture was limited but with sleek, modern lines on wide-plank wood floors. His small kitchen even had granite countertops and light-colored cabinets. The sun shone into the room from large front windows. He had a work area in one corner that took up a quarter of the open room. The desk was simple, and there weren't any places to store things. He didn't keep paper and utilized a technical process for work. It seemed efficient and uncluttered. There were two chairs in the corner that looked like they were for clients. Overall, it was a relaxing place that exuded a positive feeling.

"Can I get you something? Coffee, tea, coconut water?" Oliver asked.

I was surprised he made the offer since it didn't seem like something a tech-oriented millennial would naturally do with a guest.

"No, thanks, I'm all set. I like this apartment. Do you live here as well?"

"Yeah, I moved in here two years ago and have done some of

the renovations myself. A friend owns the house. It's in a dicey neighborhood but the rent is very reasonable, and I like it. Plus, I really don't go anywhere anyway."

He moved over to the desk and I followed him after throwing my coat on one of the chairs. I was focused on getting started and excited to see what he had put together. He turned around, walked back over, and moved my coat to a rack at the top of the stairs. I noticed a slight tremor in his hand while he raised his arm to hang it on the hook. It seemed strange in someone so young. Maybe I was just too preoccupied with health issues these days. I turned away and pretended not to notice what he was doing behind me. He came back and sat down at the desk.

"OK, let me show you the screen-by-screen sequence that I came up with for Friendly Neighbors. My main goal—as you had stressed—was to keep it super easy for the end user, which is an older individual. We can make any adjustments, and from this model, you can easily get a prototype developed."

He showed me the rough sketch of all the screens that would be needed to walk both the clients and the partners through the application. He had it laid out almost exactly as I had pictured it in my head. I did make a few slight adjustments to the services menu. There were still some details to be worked out on a mapping companion, but that could be planned later. All in all, Oliver had done a very thorough job on the wireframe project.

"Wow, Oliver, this is great and virtually painless. It seems that you've captured the vision and laid it out well. It seems very workable."

"Well, you gave me a thorough starting point, and frankly, I can see the idea and the mission. I think it has potential. Believe me when I tell you that I have seen a lot of ideas in the past few years. Not all of them are good," he laughed and quickly saved the data that we'd just adjusted. "I can send this all over to you. If you don't mind me asking, what's your next step for this?"

"I really want to get in front of some funding, since this can get expensive. I'm trying to get on the IdeaLab presentation schedule in Detroit next month." I turned to grab my coat. "If I get some funding, I want to get a working prototype created."

"IdeaLab is a great start. I've worked with them before. If you want, I can put together a deck and some storyboards for the presentation."

"Oh man, that would be a huge help! Wow, Oliver, I didn't know that you did that, too. Yes, that would be great."

I glanced over and noticed he was actually smiling. It was the kind of smile from someone who felt inner pride with the work they had just completed and the thought of being able to provide additional help. It was the look of someone who felt needed. It struck me as very endearing, especially because I knew he had experience and obvious talent. It propelled me to ask a personal question. "If you don't mind me asking since I didn't look you up on LinkedIn, what's your background? You're so talented. Where'd you go to school?"

He looked at his computer screen and seemed to be contemplating an answer. I immediately felt as if I was prying, but he then said, "I actually went to Penn State and got my BS in Software Engineering. My family lives in Erie, Pennsylvania. I came to Michigan right after college for a job with Chrysler. I eventually left there to open a small firm with two other partners where we focused solely on developing mobile apps. It went great, and we had a lot of success."

He stopped at this point, and it looked like that may be the end of the discussion. This way of talking was confusing to me and I had encountered it with him before. He seemed like he was done talking but it didn't seem natural, almost mid-thought. I had to fill the void, so I said, "That's amazing. Is the firm still in business?" The minute it was out of my mouth, I regretted the question. It was the kind of question that can make people feel bad and I knew it. His answer seemed rehearsed, like he had crafted it in some group therapy session and spun it out for friends and family when he needed to address the elephant in the room.

"Yes, it's still in business and doing very well, just not with me. I spent most of my twenties pretty much addicted to painkillers and a few other things, and it eventually ruined my relationships. I'm in recovery now, but it has been a long road."

I was stunned and embarrassed that this stranger just told me something so personal. The mother in me fought the urge to go over and give him a hug.

He must have noticed the look on my face and added, "Don't worry, it helps me to be honest with people, even people I've just met." He relaxed, and for some reason, that alone eased my embarrassment.

"Well, I'm very impressed and am so grateful that you're able to help me through this. If I can add some honesty as well, I don't know what the fuck I'm doing." We both laughed.

After a few more minutes of discussion and follow-up on the project, I headed out the door. We planned to meet again the following week to look at the presentation materials. As I drove home, I decided to check on my mom; I knew she had a dentist appointment that day with my neighbor and good friend, Sarah, our family dentist. The snow had been light but consistent, so I wanted to make sure she was OK. She didn't answer her home phone, so I tried her cell. No answer there either. The appointment had been for 1:00 and it was 3:00 now, so I assumed she would be back at home.

I called Sarah's office to see if I could catch her between patients. Her receptionist knew my name from seeing me there many times—as a patient and just for lunch—so she immediately put me through to her.

"Hey, Sarah. How's your day going?"

"Hi, Julie. What's happening?"

"I just tried to call Suz, and she didn't answer. I hope the appointment went OK today."

"Sorry, I planned to call you when I got caught up. She never showed. Is she all right? I checked with reception and she never called to cancel or reschedule, so I thought it was a little unusual."

"Oh, shit, now I'm really worried. Sorry about that, Sarah. I'm going to head to her house and see if I can find out what's happening. I'll call you later."

"Yes, keep me posted, OK?"

I hung up with Sarah and tried Mom at home again. This time she picked up on the third ring and ever-so-normally said hello.

"Oh my gosh, Mom, I'm freaking out. I talked to Sarah and she said you didn't make it to the appointment today."

"Oh, yeah, I meant to cancel but was too busy trying to help Danette. She was having trouble with her van and needed to get her kids to their activities."

"What do you mean? You ended up taking her kids somewhere?"

Danette was my mom's next-door neighbor. I had met her a few times in the front yard, and once when I stopped over and she was in my mom's living room. She was going through a divorce and confided in Mom a lot about her issues and money problems. I would guess she was about thirty-four, and she homeschooled three unruly kids. She was taking classes to become a massage therapist. Danette was also a devoted Mormon. I knew too much about Danette because my mom repeated most of their conversations to me, the most recent one being about special Mormon underwear. According to Mom, Danette purchased her underwear from a Mormon website, and they were very prudish, like granny panties. Danette told her the underwear provided protection and helped her resist temptation. I wasn't sure how much temptation was in Danette's life, but these panties sounded like the old theory of not shaving your legs before a date. Maybe Dr. Humpy could use some of those panties.

"Well, Danette came over here right before I planned to leave for Sarah's office and needed help with getting her kids to the community center," Mom said. "I couldn't just ignore her."

"Where did you have to take them? Hopefully not too far. This weather has been crazy all day. I'm not familiar with this community center. Where is it?"

"Umm, I don't know. Somewhere near the junior high over on Carlton Street," she mumbled.

"Mom, did you drive, or did Danette use your car?"

"Oh, yeah, I loaned her the car. Did I not mention that?"

"Oh, OK. Did she bring it back?"

"Umm yes, it's in the garage."

"How is she going to pick them up? Will she need to borrow it again today?"

"That is a lot of questions, Julie! I guess I'll find out when she comes to my door," she said, annoyed.

There was a long pause and I felt like this conversation wasn't making a whole lot of sense.

"Mom, what the hell. Are you sure you're OK?" It was quiet on the other end for a few seconds and then I could hear the soft, low shudders of crying.

"Oh no, what's wrong? I'm sorry if I am making you upset, Mom." I suddenly felt terrible. That was twice today that I assumed the position of the asshole in a conversation.

"Julie, it's not you. I need to tell you what really happened today, but I'm scared."

Another excruciatingly long pause. She started slowly, trying to control her emotions. "I made all of that BS up about Danette and her kids. I headed off on time for the appointment at Sarah's office. I know I've been there a few times since she moved to the new location. I knew exactly where it was, but for some strange reason, I couldn't find it. I drove around for a long time and finally pulled off the road by the mall and gave up. It was like someone had rearranged the streets. I sat there and cried and then somehow, some way, I got back home. The whole thing was like a horrible dream and I really had no idea where I was. Nothing looked familiar to me. It really scared me."

She was sobbing now, and I wanted to climb through the phone. I was still about fifteen minutes from her house, which seemed like forever. My initial reaction was to downplay the event. "Oh, Mom, that's OK, you just got a little confused is all. I'm not sure that you've been to the new office more than once or twice. It is kind of hard to find since it's tucked behind that busy shopping district."

"It *is* a little tucked away. I guess I panicked a little bit." She had pulled it together now and seemed to be rationalizing more than reacting. Maybe telling me had helped her calm down.

"I'm close to your house, so I am going to stop in. I'm also going to make a quick call to Sarah because she's worried."

"Please don't tell her what really happened!"

"I won't. I'll give her some excuse."

I hung up the phone and left a message for Sarah with her receptionist. Then I called Kylie.

Chapter 13
The Visit

KYLIE HAD BEEN BUSY since the holidays. She was promoted to a sales director position that required a lot of travel. She was gone every other week and liked the change. Her new job required her to manage a sales team, so we had lots of discussions about the daily challenges of managing people. Also, she had met someone new and the relationship was moving along nicely. His name was Ryan, and he was two years older than her. He lived in Denver and was an entrepreneur who had just started a line of men's grooming products. He was getting them featured in salons around Colorado and branching out into other states. They had met in the visitor center during a concert at Red Rocks Amphitheatre that featured some local bands. He reached for an hors d'oeuvre at the same time she did, and they soon were dating. It really was an old-fashioned "meet cute" instead of a typical "swipe right" hookup. I had not met him yet but had seen photos on social media. Nice-looking guy: I could see the attraction. I planned to get out there for my usual Mother's Day weekend visit in May to make my assessment.

Kylie answered on the last ring just as I was getting worried that I might have to leave yet another useless voicemail.

"Hi, Mom. How are you?"

"Hi, Boo," I said, using a name from her toddler days that had stuck after all these years. "I've been better. Today has been kind of a bust."

"Oh no, what's going on?"

I explained the situation with her grandma.

"Oh no, Mom, that sounds bad. What in the hell is going on?"

"I don't know, honey. I feel like all of this is related somehow, but it just doesn't make any sense. There is an MRI scheduled for next week to see what's happening with her throat, but I don't know how this fits into that problem. I'm really concerned and, yes, I'll say it, scared."

"Well, I booked my flight this morning and I'm glad I did. I'm scared, too. I'll be there in two days. I land at 4:00 p.m. You haven't told her yet, have you?"

"No, I didn't want to ruin the surprise. She'll be so excited to see you. Also, you can go to the MRI with us. Will you be able to stay until Valentine's Day?"

"Yes, I plan to leave on the 15th. Let's show her a nice time while I'm there and cheer her up!"

"That's the plan, my girl. Let's figure out a fun way to surprise her."

"OK! It'd be awesome to sneak up on her at a restaurant if you can get her out. We can talk tomorrow."

When I arrived at my mom's house, the mood was somber. She had been crying. Winnie was sulking on the sofa and didn't even try to jump on me. I walked right to Mom and gave her a long embrace.

"What did you tell Sarah?" she asked.

"I didn't have to tell her anything since she was with a patient. But I'm sure she'll want to know something when we talk next time."

"Oh, Jule, what the hell is going on with me? I'm really starting to think I have a brain tumor."

We stood perfectly still, and I shook my head. At that moment, we both knew what was happening. She was referring to her sister, Catherine. "Kink" was her nickname. Kink had passed away almost twenty-five years earlier from a malignant brain tumor. Suz and

Kink were inseparable. They were Irish twins, born eleven months apart, and loved each other dearly. The illness was devastating, and her suffering was immense. In the end, she participated in an experimental chemotherapy program where they shot drugs directly into her head. This was years ago, and treatments have come a long way since then. That program left her like a vegetable but alive for a while and in need of intensive care. My mom took care of her on many occasions near the end. She also spent a lot of time at her house caring for her three boys—my cousins—as well. It was agonizing, and it took Mom an awfully long time to deal with the loss.

"Mom, that's not at all like what you're experiencing. She had extreme headaches for months before she was diagnosed. Also, she had vision problems, too, remember?"

"You're right, but what the hell is wrong with me?"

"That's what we're going to find out, but we need to stay realistic and positive, OK? I've also been thinking that a change of scenery might be good for you. Why don't you come and stay at our house?"

"Oh, great. Now I can't live alone, is that what you think?"

"Umm, no, not what I was thinking at all, just thought it might be fun to have you at our house right now. We could do a lot of activities you like—movies, shopping, watching horrible reality shows, things to keep you busy while we sort this all out. Mark is all in and said he insists."

"Julie, I can't do that. I need to stay in my own house. Maybe I could come over for long weekends. Can we compromise?"

"I'll take that. Since it's Thursday though, why don't we pack up a few things and head over tonight? Mark wants to take us out to dinner and the guest room is all set. You like that king-sized bed upstairs."

"OK, that sounds nice. I'll go pack a bag. Can you get Winnie's things together?"

"Yup, I'll get on it. Where do you keep the dog tranquilizers?"

"Ha-ha, missy! She isn't that bad," Mom shouted as she headed down the hall to her room.

When she was out of sight, I texted Mark since I hadn't had a chance to call him yet. *Hey Mister, it's been a weird day. Bringing Mom home with me. Having her stay for a few days. Will catch you up tonight but not good :(Let's go out to dinner. Love you.*

He responded within seconds. *Oh no. Of course. See you soon. Love you.*

I got her settled in the guest room upstairs and put Winnie's dog bed in there as well. I grabbed some fresh towels from the hall linen closet and turned down the comforter. I wanted her to feel so welcome that she didn't want to leave. This would be my goal over the next few days. I was very excited about Kylie coming into town and knew that would cheer her up. Now I just needed to keep her distracted until Saturday evening when we could surprise her at the restaurant.

Kylie and I had it all planned. I would take Mom to her favorite, Olive Garden, and Kylie would surprise us while we ate. I wasn't sure how it would all go down, but Kylie had it worked out. Mom had no idea that she would be there, so it should be fun.

The weekend was going well, and Mark and I had managed to keep her busy with episodes of *Little Women of California*, a ridiculous reality show about little people and their big lives. She also loved all the home makeover shows on HGTV. To pass the time, we went to a movie and a florist to pick up some of her favorite flowers. They were in a vase on her bedside table, and the sweet scent filled her room. She was having a good time, and I think she had almost forgotten about the incident a few days earlier. It was late Saturday afternoon when I suggested we head to Olive Garden for dinner. Mark made an excuse why he couldn't join us since he knew Kylie was already in town planning her ambush. Also, he was not a fan of the Garden; even unlimited pasta bowls could not lure him there.

The atmosphere was energetic with families crammed into

booths chatting about their day and waitresses scurrying by to help them get all the salad and garlic breadsticks they could possibly handle. We settled into a booth and ordered drinks. Mom was talking about Kent's house, which I had never been to. It was a new build in a great part of town. She had a photo on her phone. It was a gorgeous home with a stone and brick façade and lots of windows. My mom said he had beautiful furniture done by a designer, and a lap pool. It was a big house for a single guy, but he had his extended family over quite often. She mentioned that he wanted to have us all over for dinner one of these days.

She used this comment to turn the conversation around. "Speaking of family, have you talked to Kylie lately? I haven't heard from her in a week. What the hell is going on?"

"I haven't talked to her much either, Mom. I know she's been busy with the new job and, of course, Ryan. He's the new boyfriend, you know."

"Oh, yeah, I can't wait to hear all about the new guy. When do you think we'll see the little snoot?"

"Last time I talked to her, we were trying to come up with a time she can visit, so hopefully soon," I added as I forked one of the appetizers. I wanted to shun the carb-heavy sampler platter, but it was calling to me like an old friend.

Mom gave me a shoulder shrug and a frown and just then, Kylie appeared behind her with a bouquet of flowers. Mom couldn't see her, and I felt a zap of electricity as I struggled to get my phone out to take a video of the surprise. I was fumbling and, as it turned out, barely managed to get a photo.

"Is this seat taken, ma'am?" Kylie asked.

Mom looked over her shoulder and her eyes bulged. She moved to the far end of the booth to see more clearly. "Oh my God! Oh my God! Oh my God! What is going on?" Her eyes were tearing up and people at the other tables were watching us.

"Kylie, that was so right on cue, you have no idea!" I gasped through my own tears.

She came in for a hug. "Here I am, Grandma. The bitch is back."

We were all laughing and crying. It had gone perfectly. I could see the total joy for all three of us as we were reunited right there at that beautiful Olive Garden. We talked and laughed for the next two hours and then headed back to my house. My mom could not believe that Kylie was staying for a week and that we had pulled off an amazing surprise. That night, I would have bet that whatever was nagging her was long gone and she was herself again.

The week ahead was full of fun, and the trio was fully engaged. We stayed up late and watched horrible television shows and our favorite movies. Mom made us pour over her reputable news sources: *People*, *Star*, and *National Enquirer*. We talked about everyone and everything and laughed nonstop. At one point, we pulled out a massive box of old photos and got my mom's commentary on many of the pictures.

"You see, Ky, your mom was a very fat baby. I'm not sure why, since I fed her exactly like I fed Jeffrey, but she just kept getting plumper. I think she may have a good amount of natural fat cells and that could be why. See her here, she takes up this entire wagon."

"Mom, that's not fair, that picture is just a bad angle and an extremely small wagon! And I do think you pushed the food into my face because you have a secret obsession with fat baby knees and elbows."

"Yes, Grams, I remember a video at Dad's house of you going ape shit over my fat knees and elbows as a baby. You would tickle them by blowing raspberries with your mouth." She stopped to demonstrate, including a high-pitched voice! "Thank God Mom never left you in charge of my nutrition. Can you imagine the number of spin classes I'd need?"

We teased her about starting all our names with the letter "J"— *so* original. She claimed it was a complete accident. First, there was Jeffrey and then her favorite girl's name was Julie. It wasn't until then that she noticed they were both J's and had to keep the pattern.

SOMETIMES SHELLS MAKE SAND

Kylie gave us the lowdown on Ryan and how the whole relationship was going. Not a full picture, but a few choice tidbits. There were also some comments about Kent in that area. We did each other's hair and makeup and mocked each other's outfits. Poor Mark just tried to stay out of the way and maintain his sanity. I noticed Winnie got plenty of walks with her new friend Mark.

We went to the MRI, which was uneventful since they still needed someone to interpret the results. Mom needed a mild sedative because of being in the tube with her claustrophobia, but it went quickly, and she was fine afterward. They sent the results to Dr. Manning and the new doctor, a neurologist, who we would see the following week. Hopefully, this would give us some much-needed information.

Kylie and I also went over to Oliver's house to review the updated wireframe panels and the presentation tools. It was all impressive, and Kylie was very taken with Oliver's talents. I didn't tell her about the opioid addiction as it didn't enter the equation. She thought the Friendly Neighbors app idea was shaping up to be something that may have a chance of catching on.

"So, Oliver, you're telling me that this whole concept was my mom's idea? Or be honest, did you shape it a bit and give it some of the details? Tech isn't really something I'd think is her strong suit."

"Hey, Ky, I'm actually standing right here and can hear you," I whispered loudly.

"I wish I could take some credit for the concept, but it was all your mom." There was a long pause in which it seemed to be the end of the thought but wasn't. "I think she may be onto something that has a target market and usability."

Kylie gave me a glance that indicated she noticed the weird cadence of Oliver's speech pattern. "Wow, I can actually say I'm impressed, Mom. This is really great, and I'm excited for you!"

I'd gotten the impression that she wasn't so sure of that fact before we went to Oliver's.

103

Valentine's Day came too soon, and Kylie was leaving the next day. We decided to dress in pink or red pajamas and have a beautiful candlelight dinner in the dining room, just the four of us. We had little gifts for each other wrapped in red paper or placed in pink foil gift bags. Mark had sent us all roses that day and was preparing a special dinner. Kent and Ryan had also managed to send their ladies flowers, too. The table looked beautiful, bathed in candlelight with multiple vases of all kinds of gorgeous flowers scattered down the middle among the candles.

One of my favorite photos of all time came out of that night. Mark was slow dancing with my mom in the dining room to Nat King Cole's "Unforgettable." She looked so happy in her pink, two-piece pajamas with the large, colorful hearts. Her eyes were slightly closed, she had a sweet smile, and she looked happy again—truly unforgettable.

I was in a rut after Kylie left and needed an attitude change. Mom had decided to go home as well, so the house was quiet. The issues with my mom were weighing on me heavily, and I had used the visit as a distraction from all the unknowns. We had an upcoming appointment with a new doctor, a neurologist, to give us feedback on the MRI images. I figured they must not be that serious since Dr. Manning had seen them and didn't call or ask us to come into her office. I might have been reading too many positive ideas into that outcome, but that is what I needed.

Chapter 14
The Recovery

FILLING OUT THE APPLICATION for IdeaLab was just the perfect distraction. I was putting it off but had to get it done to make the submission deadline for the next jury meeting. The jury was a group of technology do-gooders who decided which ideas could move on to be heard by pre-approved investors.

I opened my laptop at the kitchen table and stared at the website. It claimed that the mission of IdeaLab was to connect business technology ideas to investors and resources. It also stated their goal was to promote economic development and the creation of jobs. These both sounded nice. I knew there was a bunch of foundation money from very wealthy donors that got thrown in a pot to support growth. It must be nice to be super rich and work so hard to find new and interesting ways to spend your mountains of cash and get tax breaks at the same time. No problem here, I'd take a piece of the mountain to help Friendly Neighbors move along. I dug into the application and spent time contemplating my answers to these questions:

What is the problem you are trying to solve?

How can your idea better lives?

How can your idea promote job growth?

How can your idea positively change the community?

I had the questions nailed because the whole concept of Friendly Neighbors was to connect people who needed help with someone in their community who was looking to make money in their spare time and could provide help. Seemed like a slam dunk (trying to stay confident). I finished all the components and sent the email.

The next step was for a jury to review the submissions and choose five worthy finalists. The finalists would be invited to present in-person, and then, based on the feedback of the jury panel, sent to meet with potential investors. This portion of the project felt remarkably similar to what I used to do for a living—making presentations and trying to generate revenue was right in my wheelhouse. I'd heard the competition could be stiff; I went in with my usual confidence but tempered it slightly as this was out of my comfort zone.

With that off my list, I needed to get together a battle plan, considering what we might find out from the neurologist the next day. There was obviously something wrong with my mom. She was continuing to lose weight and had trouble sometimes with swallowing and balance. We had considered all the possibilities, but the brain tumor idea seemed to be the worst and possibly the most probable. I started to think about how we would handle that diagnosis; I feel better when I'm making an action plan even for horrible scenarios. I braced myself and planned for the worst but hoped for the best.

The neurologist was about forty years old and wore very casual clothes and no white coat. Dr. Krill was associated with Metrix Hospital and had been recommended by one of our neighbors who worked there as an ER doctor. I had discussed my mom's case with him one evening at a neighborhood cocktail party. He listened intently and then gently touched my shoulder and said, "Critical weight loss is never a good sign if it can't be explained. I would get your mom to some new specialists."

His words had sent a shock down my spine. This discussion basically undid all the positive effects of all three vodka and sodas. He was being serious, and I knew it. He then said he would email me some recommendations. Dr. Krill was at the top of his list and took our appointment immediately.

He seemed like a very personable guy and mentioned that he had been phoned by my neighbor on our behalf. He had already studied the MRI films and proceeded to give my mom a typical exam, checking reflexes and strength in the arms and legs. He also observed her eye tracking and several other things. I was extremely anxious as he went through this series of tests since I knew he had already looked at the information. Finally, he sat back down on his stool.

"There have been a series of mild strokes, and I believe that is causing the swallowing and mobility issues with you, Suzanne." He went on to explain a lot of medical jargon while he showed us the scans. But the bottom line was that her current health issues could all be related to the mild strokes. He also said he thought that through various rehabilitation programs, she would have the potential to recover. RECOVER. This hung in the air as Mom turned toward me and smiled.

"So, do you think I can get back to my old self?"

"With speech therapy, you have the potential to regain control in your throat muscles. I also think that with some physical therapy and mobility exercises, you can get better with your balance. But there will be some residual effects, so getting back to 100 percent will be a challenge."

"So, I can feel better than this and the swallowing can be improved," she asked slowly.

"I would like you to get an evaluation with a speech pathologist and a physical therapist to give you a better idea of the recovery options. I will get Dr. Manning my findings and recommendations. I'm sure they will be in touch with you soon for the next steps."

"Dr. Krill, is there a danger of any more of these strokes? How long ago did these occur? Can you tell?" I asked.

"It looks like these are older, possibly in the last year, and no, there is no way to guarantee that there will never be another episode. It is best if you can recognize the warning signs. I have all of that information here and will send it home with you."

With that, he handed me a pamphlet and asked Mom if she had any more questions. We were both taking it all in and didn't have any at the moment. Dr. Krill said to schedule a follow-up appointment at the desk.

In the car on the way home, we talked about the past year and times when the strokes may have occurred. Of course, there was Christmas Day when she passed out, and the day she got lost in the car. That would answer many questions. But for some reason, the fact that her weight loss started well before those incidents really bothered me. I didn't want to say anything to her because she seemed relieved by this diagnosis, and frankly, I was, too.

Dr. Manning phoned the next day and went over the follow-up appointments that were scheduled with the speech pathologist and physical therapist in the next few weeks.

I called my brothers and sister in the meantime to let them know what we had learned at Dr. Krill's. I went through the materials he had given us on stroke recovery and was a little concerned about some of the information. There was a good possibility she would have other strokes. Depending on the severity, this could result in her losing more mobility and even potentially becoming bedridden. I felt like it was time we came up with a family plan. Jeff supplied a conference line number from work, and we agreed to get on the call the next night to discuss our concerns. We were all having a hard time thinking about a future with Mom's health conditions. Everyone was in denial since she had seemed healthy just a few months before. Yes, she could recover and begin eating more and walking better, but what if she didn't and, worse yet, what if she had more strokes? We decided that for now, she would stay in her house and we would divide and conquer. Jon would check on some of the emergency services, like LifeCall, in case something happened to her. I would try to get her to come to my house on the weekends and take her to the doctor and therapy appointments. Jenny would come to town for a visit and go with us to the first speech therapy meeting. Jeff would check her budget numbers just to make sure she was OK financially in case she wanted some in-home help at some point. We were going to recommend a housekeeper starting next week. We knew Mom was in charge and would never let us decide anything that had to do with her lifestyle, but it was good to have a plan anyway.

Jenny arrived in town and went to stay at Mom's house. She was able to be there for the next two days, so Mom was excited about the visit. Day one would be busy with the speech therapy appointment. I drove the three of us to the medical center and we went in and met with the speech language pathologist. She was short, dishwater-blonde, and very businesslike. She seemed to take her job seriously and had a no-nonsense approach. She was nice enough but wanted to get right to the meat of the appointment. Jen and I tried to introduce ourselves, but she turned right to Mom.

"Hi, Suzanne. I understand that you're having some speech and swallowing problems related to some strokes. Is that correct?"

Mom nodded and looked at Jenny and me for backup. I could already tell she wasn't getting a good vibe.

"First off, Suzanne," she interrupted our glances, "you're going to need to talk as much as you can. Use it or lose it, I always tell my patients. Your tongue is a muscle and if it gets weak, it will not work properly."

Great. Mom was already skeptical about speech therapy and now we have this woman barking orders like Dorinda in the Berkshires.

"Yes, I've been having some speech and swallowing issues. Some days are better than others, but I do want to improve," Mom said very sweetly. This surprised Jen and me since we were expecting a spat of obscenities. Maybe this would work after all.

"Great, let's go through some exercises, and I can evaluate your therapy plan," she said.

She motioned for Mom to sit in the chair at a small table and for Jen and me to go to the chairs along the wall. First off, she went through the normal health questions and asked about her swallowing problems. After having her say certain words and make certain sounds, she made some notes in the file she had lying on the table. She then left the room to get some food samples for further evaluation.

Mom looked at us and slightly slurred, "Great, girls. This chick is a real bitch. I think I actually might stab her in the neck."

"Mom, what the hell. She's doing her job and trying to help!" Jen whispered loudly.

The exchange was cut short once the woman breezed back into the room. We couldn't really tell if she had heard us. She was down to business, a very cool cucumber, and not easily rattled. For some people, that may seem like a disturbing conversation to overhear, but for us, it was normal.

She was now focused on a handful of small containers of different foods and liquids. "I want to evaluate your swallowing and will use an endoscopic assessment so I can watch you swallow on screen." She held up a tube with a small light on it and moved to place it on the end of my mom's nose. "Don't worry; it won't hurt at all," she said. "It will just help us to see how the swallowing is actually occurring in your throat."

After attaching the tube, she had Mom drink water and juice. From there, she had her eat a variety of things like applesauce, pudding, macaroni and cheese, and some solid foods. All the while, she watched it on the screen as Mom slowly chewed and eventually swallowed. Finally, she had seen enough.

"Well, it seems that your throat is working properly. You do hesitate at the pharyngeal phase when the food moves down to the throat. And I don't see anything going into the airway, so it seems to be functioning OK. Does it feel like food can go into your airway, and is that what is causing your hesitation?"

"It does sometimes feel like I could choke, which makes me

not want to swallow." Mom was slurring her words a little more than usual today and seemed tired from this process.

"I'm going to give you some material with tips for eating. Also, I want you to focus on soft foods and eating small meals more often. If you chew with your chin down, it will help." She demonstrated the position. "No more than thirty-minute meal sessions because any longer fatigues the muscles. Also, we need to up the caloric intake. There is a powder you can mix into your soft foods to increase calories. It's called Benecalorie, and you can get it at the drugstore. You can also try Magic Cup, Ensure, and Boost pudding. All the food information is in the packet." She handed it to me, and I started to look through the material. She had gone through all of that quickly, so I was sure I would need to reference the information later.

"Let's set up the next four appointments," she said.

We got out our calendars and picked four times. After we had those set in all our devices, she casually added, "I have two concerns at this time. One is getting food into your airway, which can cause pneumonia. Practice coughing while pushing on a hard surface to clear your windpipe if needed. The second is turning your weight loss around. If that does not happen quickly, you will need a feeding tube." And before we could even comprehend what she just said, she quickly closed with, "I'll see you late next week, Suzanne." Then she picked up her files and motioned us toward the door.

The room fell silent. A feeding tube? Where did that come from? We were there to get her on the road to recovery, not to consider drastic measures! I was immediately pissed and knew Jenny and Mom must be, too. She didn't offer anything more though, and we filed out in silence. We were still mulling over that last comment when we got settled in the car.

"Feeding tube? What the hell is that all about?" Mom sputtered.

"She doesn't have the best bedside manner, does she?" I said. "I think she just says things out loud without realizing that it may startle the patient. She's basically a twat."

"Exactly," Jen added. "She didn't realize that was weird because she's an ass, so let's just let it go."

"I don't feel comfortable with her and I'm not sure I can work with the dumb ass twat."

"Now, Mom, let's just give her a chance to see if she can help. If this works, it'll get you on the road to recovery from the strokes. Who cares what she's like if the process helps?"

My mom gave me an eye roll and I returned a weak smile.

Chapter 15
The Presentation

JEN NEEDED TO RETURN TO her five-ring circus before her house burned down from unsupervised mayhem, and that left Mom and me to plan the next steps.

"I think it would be fun if you could come and hang out over the weekend, Mom."

"Oh Jule, I have so much to do at home. I haven't vacuumed in a while and the kitchen needs some organizing."

"Mom, you keep forgetting that we hired a service to take care of house cleaning. They're coming tomorrow to do all of that stuff."

"Yes, I know, but I need to clean up a little first. I don't want them to think I'm a total slob."

"Cleaning before the cleaning service doesn't make much sense. Let's just gamble on the idea that they might be offended by your disgusting home and let it go." We both laughed since we knew her house was already extremely clean.

"Also, I need your help in critiquing my presentation for Friendly Neighbors as I'm one of five finalists and the presentation is scheduled for Wednesday."

"Sure, I'll help you and I promise to only give constructive criticism. I won't mention anything about your hair, clothes, or tone of voice—nothing like that, probably not helpful."

I also wanted to be able to help her with the new diet, so getting a few meals organized would be a start. I knew we would need to figure out a different bedroom for her since getting up and down our stairs was precarious for her. Mark suggested we turn the workout room on the main floor into a guest room. This would avoid stairs and be just around the corner from the master bedroom. There was also a full bath just outside the door. Although she didn't want us to go to any trouble, I could tell she was relieved about the switch. Mark worked on changing the furniture, and we had it all set by the time she arrived on Friday.

Mom liked to relax watching TV in our family room and was trying to get through some *Game of Thrones*. She seemed really into it except for all the medieval family names and some of the graphic scenes that made her shudder. The scenes with Ramsey and his torture tactics were particularly distasteful, as was the hand chop for poor Jamie. Winnie was both relaxed and stimulated at our house. She slept on her dog bed part of the day and enjoyed crashing through the woods chasing chipmunks, squirrels, and rabbits. The lab part of her Labradoodle wanted to hunt but didn't seem to know why.

All in all, we had a great couple of days. I also talked her into trying some of the recommended foods for increasing calories, and she practiced the chin tuck while chewing.

"This chin-tucking thing is really kind of stupid. I feel like my tongue is still in the way and this whole BS is just supposed to distract me from the thought of choking to death."

"I think it may be helping, Mom, and anything to be able to swallow more will help to put some weight back on."

"It actually feels a little better if I stand while I try it. Can you imagine eating in a restaurant while I stand at the end of the table trying to swallow? Ridiculous."

We changed her to slowly drinking through a straw for all liquids, and she complained all along the way. However, I felt a little relieved to think there may be some light at the end of this tunnel if we could make progress.

I had a long conversation with Kylie on Saturday while Mom

took a nap. Kylie, like me, was not convinced that the strokes were the sole cause of my mom's health issues. We bounced around a few ideas and searched the web for symptoms but came up with nothing new except human immunodeficiency virus (HIV). Since that wasn't it, we decided to stay with the current therapy route. I promised to keep Kylie updated on the progress.

Later that day, Oliver stopped over to deliver the presentation materials and discuss the flow for Tuesday. I had asked him to become involved, and he was happy to assist based on the potential to get in on the ground floor. We hadn't talked about anything solid in the way of revenue sharing, which seemed very premature. For now, I was paying his consulting rate. I was grateful for his help because I felt like a fifty-year-old in the land of the twenty-somethings. We spoke different languages: I was Ms. Pac-Man to his Fortnite, but we made it work when it came to the project.

In the IdeaLab document that was sent to me after my application, they explained that we would have twenty minutes to present the idea. We could use any type of presentation materials and were given free rein, only limited by our imaginations and IdeaLab's office space. We had some PowerPoint slides and a few visual pieces of the software wireframe set up. We also had a video from some potential clients that explained how this could enhance their lives. These were victims from our mall survey who were happy to get on camera. We steered clear of asking Frank (Mr. Conspiracy Theory) to do the video since he was a loose cannon when given the floor. I practiced the pitch until I had it down to about eighteen minutes. I felt confident that I could get through it smoothly. Oliver gave me a few tips about what the jury wanted to hear, and we fine-tuned the main points.

I also practiced it a few times for Oliver, Mark, and my mom as the audience.

"I think the idea makes sense and if it matters at all, you should wear your hair up since it makes you look more intelligent and less frizzy."

"Thanks, Mom, super helpful."

"You are going to kill it, baby. I think you're ready to get this done." Mark was positive as he gave me a fist bump.

"Hey, Oliver, would you like to stay for dinner? We're having pasta with my famous marinara sauce," Mark asked.

"Wow, I would love to stay, thank you." He paused and Mark started to speak when Oliver finally added, "I don't cook very much. I mostly order in, so that sounds really good."

Mark regrouped and continued his thought, "I've been perfecting this recipe for years and it's always a fan favorite. Probably eat in about an hour, is that OK with everyone?"

"I'm starving so the sooner, the better, but I can make some cheese and crackers. Mom, would you like a little something right now?" I asked.

"A glass of wine would be perfect for me. I can skip the food. Oliver, would you like some wine?" Mom asked.

Oliver looked at Mom and declined the wine but asked for a glass of water. This got her wheels turning. "You don't drink, Oliver?"

"I love to drink—especially good wine—but it's not part of my recovery," he said, glancing over at her casually.

I had filled Mom in on Oliver, but she must have forgotten what I had told her. She was usually overly sensitive to people who were struggling with addiction or mental health challenges.

Suz studied him and must have finally remembered. "I should actually refrain as well since I can barely swallow the stuff anyway. It may impact the enjoyment of dinner if there's red wine dripping down my chin all evening," she said.

We all laughed and with that moved on to all kinds of conversation. Oliver let it slip that he was engaged and would be getting married in June.

"That's fantastic! Congratulations, Oliver! Where's the wedding?" I asked, avoiding the use of a pronoun because I didn't know the sex of his intended. It could be a man or a woman; I didn't know Oliver well enough and certainly didn't want to assume.

Mark was also trying to be diplomatic, "So exciting, what kind of wedding are you having? Big or small?"

"We plan to get married by the water in Traverse City. We both love it up there and it will be family and some friends, not too big."

We still didn't know if Oliver was marrying a male or female until Suz got to the point. "Who are you marrying and how did you meet?"

"Hailey is a former client, and we've been seeing each other for two years. She's amazing." (Long pause, but it seemed there was more to come, so we waited.) "We have a lot of things in common, and I'm incredibly lucky."

Oliver was such an accomplished and sweet person but also seemed so vulnerable. I found myself wanting to support him and see him win. It was comforting to have him in my corner.

Wednesday was the big day. I was nervous and excited as I picked up Oliver and drove into downtown Detroit. He might have been nervous as well because he was silent in the car, but that wasn't unusual for him. There was a good amount of traffic cruising well above the speed limit as we got closer to the city. There were also a few dilapidated and burned-out houses along the freeway from the "bad years." But these days, Detroit is being heralded as "America's Comeback City." There were new restaurants, retail stores, office buildings, and apartments everywhere you looked. The city was in quite a turnaround and the downtown area was vibrant and reborn. There were pedestrians hustling along the streets and lots of small parks and greenspace mixed in with the skyscrapers. I had not been in the city in a few years, and it was very impressive.

IdeaLab took up two floors of a building near Campus Martius Park, the center of downtown. One level was for their offices and the other was utilized for the lab space. We found the door to IdeaLab on the fourth floor. The room was large and had refinished hardwood and huge metal-rimmed windows. At the front of the room was an area for the six-panel jury to sit at a long table. There was also a screen, computer, and audio equipment. The area in front of the jury table had rows of chairs for participants, guests, and also curious visitors as this process was open to the public. The audience was full of tight suits, thick-framed glasses, a few man buns (muns), vintage shirts, brown leather Oxfords, and fashionable shoulder bags or backpacks.

"You can't swing a dead cat in here without hitting a hipster," I whispered to Oliver, hoping afterward that I didn't offend him.

We both smirked and looked around the room. "I know, what a bunch of asshats," he said, unfazed.

I went to the registration table to let them know we were here. Oliver took a seat at the end of the second row in the chairs reserved for the five presenters.

"Oh, great, you're with Friendly Neighbors," said the young woman at the registration table. She had long, straight, black hair and a small but delicate nose ring in the left nostril. "I looked at your stuff when it came through, and it really sounds interesting. I can't wait to see your presentation."

"Thanks so much. This is a little nerve-wracking. I didn't know so many people would be here," I said.

"Yeah, we get a good amount of the tech crowd at these things who are interested in what's being developed out there. Most of them are cynical and snarky, but overall, completely harmless. Just picture them in cosplay outfits since they spend a good amount of time at Comic-Con." She smiled at me, and we both laughed. "Don't worry; you'll be fine."

The session was getting started and I took my seat by Oliver. The CEO of IdeaLab, Ron Carson, welcomed everyone and spoke about the mission of IdeaLab and logistics for the morning. The more he talked, the more nervous I became. What in the fuck was I doing here? The little voices in my head were screaming to get the hell out while I still had a chance. Run, bitch, run! There was no way this idea had an inkling of hope for development. Just look at the people in this room! My panic level was rapidly approaching Mach 10. I needed to use all my skills to calm myself down. I had been nervous before—speaking at conferences or national board meetings—but this was different. These people were not my peers; I was out of my element. Just then, I felt Oliver tap my leg.

I looked over at him, and he smiled and mouthed, "You are going to slay this." He knew exactly what I was thinking. Oliver had a sixth sense about others' insecurities. I relaxed immediately and smiled back. I heard the tail end of Ron's comments and learned that I would be the third speaker out of the five.

The first presentation was by a woman with a cleaning service that would also take pets to the vet or to grooming appointments. She was well-spoken and closely resembled the overly groomed Shih Tzu she had brought as a prop. The jury seemed to like her data about working people and their pets. Then came a young couple with an idea for an online cocktail kit. It would be delivered right to your door when you wanted to throw a great themed party. There was a mimosa bar and a Bloody Mary bar with all the fixings. It seemed like a slam-dunk idea, at least for many who love a spicey Mary—but I wasn't sure the hipsters were into the idea. I looked around the room and couldn't believe that everyone was on their phones, silently opening, swiping, and clicking through to the next best thing. I couldn't tell if they liked the idea or were doing research on competitors. It really didn't matter: only the jury would decide if there were potential investors who fit the idea. The audience didn't have any power in this scenario. I made a mental note to keep that in mind as I was called up next with a short introduction.

The presentation went just as I had rehearsed many times. I used Oliver as my eye contact point since his presence gave me confidence. Halfway through, I felt the hipster audience was not interested in this idea for "old people," and I toyed with the nose-ring girl's idea of imagining them in Star Wars costumes but didn't want to get distracted. Fortunately, when I came to the data slides about smartphone usage by age, and the video endorsements, the energy in the room shifted. I think it had dawned on everyone that this was a very underserved demographic with disposable income. The light bulbs started to go on, and I could feel the interest. I made eye contact with Oliver, and he gave me a low thumbs-up. My confidence was at a high, and I ended the presentation strong. I felt like I had left nothing on the table and with the materials that Oliver had provided, this was it. If we didn't get a chance at some investors through this process, then it wasn't meant to be.

As the session ended, Ron reminded us all that they would be back in touch within the next two weeks. IdeaLab had a group of investors who would review all the ideas and match us to the opportunities that made sense. These offers could range from partial investment to full support with a team to put our idea through development. If we didn't get an investor option at this point, we could reapply after thirty days. He thanked everyone for being there and offered up pastries and a coffee bar in the back of the room.

I turned to Oliver and said, "I'm taking you to a great lunch away from here!"

"Perfect. I feel low-key twitchy since this room is a carbon copy of my former life. Let's get out of here and celebrate because you leveled up and crushed it."

We had an amazing lunch at a great seafood restaurant in Detroit. It had a beautiful view of the Detroit River and the skyline of Windsor, Ontario, across the water as well. We discussed the next steps, and I felt great. This was a point in my life where I was really going for it, and I was proud that I had put my ass on the line.

The next steps would be critical to making this dream a reality. If I struck out on getting investment interest, I didn't think we would get the prototype created, and that would be the end of the road for Friendly Neighbors. I had to be patient and wait to see what the jury decided in the next few weeks.

Early Friday morning, I woke to my cell phone ringing.

"Hi, Mom. How are you?"

There was no response, a pause, and then a very weak voice. "Julie, I'm not doing well at all. I was up and down last night and had a hard time getting out of bed the last time, and I just can't go to the speech therapy appointment today. Or even come over to spend the weekend." She started to cry.

"Oh my God, Mom. I'm coming over."

There was a long pause and then a very slurred, sobbing speech. "No, you don't need to. I'm a mess and I'm embarrassed because I wet the bed. I think I may have passed out sometime, too, because I woke up on the floor in the hall."

Trying to speak calmly but starting to cry myself, I said, "Mom, I'm coming and I'm sending Danette over right now if she's home. Stay put; it's going to be OK."

"No, don't send Danette!"

"It's OK, Mom. I just want her to stay with you until I get there. Where are you now?"

"I'm lying on the sofa."

"Stay put; I'm on my way. Keep your phone next to you so I can call you right back when I get in the car, OK?"

"OK, I will. I'm sorry." She hung up as she muffled her sobs.

I turned to Mark, who was already throwing on some clothes after hearing my side of the exchange. "Oh my God, Mark, I'm so worried. She doesn't sound good at all." The panic began to sink in as I ran to the walk-in closet, pulled a sweater over my head, and threw on some jeans.

"Baby, I know, don't worry. We'll get over there and see what we can do. Call Danette right now and see if she's home and can help. I'll start the car."

I looked up Danette in my contacts, called her, and it went to her voicemail. She was always working more than one job, and it was a longshot that she would be home. I ran to the garage and got in the car with Mark driving. "Danette didn't answer. I am going to call Suz back."

My fears heightened with each ring as I worried it might go to voicemail. She answered on the fourth ring. She didn't say anything. "Hi, Mom. How are you doing right now? We're on our way." There was no response; just some low, garbled, choking sounds. "Mom. Oh my God, Mom! Are you there?" I was now screaming.

She finally whispered, "Jule, I am ..." and then she hung up.

I immediately dialed 911.

Chapter 16
The Help

THE HIGHWAY PUT ME in a trance as I held my cell phone tightly in one hand and focused my eyes out the side window of the car. The lines and reflective markers were hypnotic, and the occasional roadkill and other debris were suddenly invisible. I didn't say anything; it seemed that a conversation would only slow us down, and we needed to get there as quickly as possible. Mark sat in silence as he navigated the freeway. I wandered off and started thinking about so many memories to keep my mind distracted.

In fourth grade, I was selected to be the May Queen at my Catholic school. This was an honor since our school was called St. Mary's, and the May Queen got to crown the huge Mary statue that watched over our playground and sprawling lawn. It was a culmination of a festival and potluck lunch where parents and students gathered for the event.

I rushed into the house after school one day. "Mom, you won't believe it, but I found out that I get to be the May Queen!"

"What did you say, Jule?" She was on the phone with the neighbor and held the receiver away with her hand.

"I was voted to be the May Queen! Isn't that great?"

"Hey Pat, I'll need to call you back, it sounds like Julie has some groundbreaking news," she said as she hung up.

"OK, tell me about this May Queen situation. It sounds very exciting."

"Every year they pick one girl from school to be the May Queen and the whole school votes on it and this year, it's me!"

"Wow, that is fantastic. What are the duties of the queen?"

"She mainly gets to crown the Virgin Mary statue with a flower wreath at the festival while everyone sings. Also, I'll read in church at the mass. It's a really big deal. I'm going to need to get a new dress since I have nothing to wear and you're supposed to dress up—not in our uniform—and can you help me do something with my hair, too?"

"When is this May Queen extravaganza?"

"It's next Thursday. Can we go shopping this weekend?"

"Julie, you know I need to go help out at Aunt Kink's this weekend. She's in a wheelchair now and the boys have no clean clothes, and I need to pack lunches and make some meals. I was hoping you could go with me and help. We can go look for a dress on Monday or Tuesday."

"But Mom, what if we can't find the right one and we run out of time? I'm going to look stupid!"

"Julie, don't start this. Some people have big problems, like your dying aunt. Let's not be selfish and cry about a dress!"

"I just wish you cared as much about me as you do about my cousins right now!"

I ran into my room, slammed the door, and cried on my bed until dinner. We didn't speak of it again and the excitement of being May Queen almost disappeared. She was mad at me for being selfish and I was mad at her for not caring about my big day, and so we didn't talk much over the next few days. I went with her to my aunt's house and made beds and prepared sandwiches like a robot. The environment was depressing; even my smart-ass cousins were quiet.

The following week sped by, and I had a rehearsal in the school garden with some of the choir and the principal. My enthusiasm was low, and I was resigned to the fact that I would probably look like an idiot and the big deal would be spoiled.

Wednesday evening after dinner, my mom called me into her room.

"Julie, I know we haven't been communicating very well, and I am sorry if you feel like I don't care about your May Queen event. I do care. All of us are going to be there, and we are proud of you. My concern is that you need to be considerate of other people's feelings sometimes. People are going through a lot in this world, and you need to learn to look beyond yourself. Do you understand?"

"Yes, I understand, and I'm sorry if I acted like a brat. I know that there are people who need our help, and it isn't always on our schedule."

"Yes, and I know Aunt Kink and Uncle Charlie and the boys appreciate everything we can do for them right now." She got out of her chair, went to her closet, and came back with a garment bag with three hanger tops sticking out of the handle.

"I picked up three dresses, and I think at least one of them might work for you. I asked some girls about your age who were shopping with their moms. They approved of all three, so hopefully, you like them."

"What, you got me three?"

"Well, I think we'll just keep your favorite, but I wanted you to have a choice."

I tried them all on and it was tough because they were all great. I finally landed on a sky-blue dress with buttons down the back and on the cuffs. It was grown-up and so pretty, and it made me feel amazing!

"Great, that's a good choice. Also, I had something else made for you. It's in the refrigerator, and I have an idea of what we can do to your hair."

I ran to the kitchen and found a gorgeous fresh flower crown. It had pink teacup roses and baby's breath and smelled delicious.

"It will look pretty if we pull up the sides and maybe put them in a loose braid, and then attach the crown right before your ceremony. What do you think, Jules?"

"Oh, wow, Mom. This is so pretty! I would have never thought of this. Thanks so much."

I remember giving her a hug that was so genuine: not only had she answered all my hopes for the next day, I also had learned something about caring for others.

A lot of memories crashed through my brain on that drive. So many ways that my mom—who was always full of smart remarks and cynical comments—had taught me life lessons.

I was a teenager who made a good number of questionable choices. One in particular was such a vivid memory about getting caught shoplifting. We lived in an upscale neighborhood and had everything, but for some reason, I liked to shoplift. It gave me a thrill and stealing clothes from Foxmoor and Hudson's really improved my wardrobe. I had also started a sort of "Shoplifting Training Program" for some of my friends who wanted to get in on the act. I had perfected a few techniques, like bringing your own shopping bag from a previous trip and cutting off tags immediately so you could always say it was yours from before. I knew where all the cameras were, and which departments and dressing rooms were the easiest to score. I had developed quite a following and amassed a good number of items, so much so that I had to give some of them away, so that my parents weren't suspicious.

One fateful day, I got cocky and greedy and was nabbed as I left the department store.

"Young lady, I'll need to look in that bag," a plainclothes security guard said as she grabbed my arm.

I pulled my arm back quickly. "Let go of me! These items are all mine."

"Well, I've been following you and saw you put that sweater in the bag."

Oh, shit. My heart sank, and I knew I had been caught. I tried to argue as she forcibly escorted me back into the store.

"Hey, my mom actually works here. I'm not sure if she's here tonight, but you should get her. She'll vouch for me."

It was a huge gamble to confess that, but I was desperate. The woman looked at me and said, "Your mom is an employee here? Who is she?"

I told her my mom's name as we entered the store office and she sat me in a chair. She emptied the bag on a desk and explained that she was store security. My face felt like it was on fire. I hoped my mom was not working, and this whole thing would just blow over. My anxiety built as I sat there for what seemed like forever while she made some calls.

"Julie, what in the hell is going on? They told me you've been shoplifting?" Mom was mad as hell and staring into my soul. There was also another security guard at the door with her.

"Mom, I came to return a few things I got last week. You remember that blazer, right?"

I motioned to a deep plum blazer with no tags that was sitting on the desk with a shirt and a sweater.

"Yes, I've seen that blazer before, but I don't know about the sweater."

The security team looked at each other, and I saw my mom get some tears in her eyes that made me start to cry as well.

The security guard said, "The sweater is what I saw her put in her bag in the fitting room. I know for sure it's stolen."

"Julie Marie, I can't believe you! You're stealing from the store where I work? This is disgusting."

"Mom, I'm so sorry. I don't know why I took that sweater. It was a big mistake." I had also stolen the shirt and the blazer but was hoping to only cop to the one item.

"You better believe it's a mistake, and one you're clearly going to regret."

"Well, it's under $50, so we'll write you up as a misdemeanor, and you'll need to appear. But we can let you go home tonight, without the sweater, since your mom is here."

After filling out some paperwork, I got into my car and headed home. I knew there would be hell to pay.

Mom came into my room and ripped me a new one, "Do you know that I could have been fired today because of your actions? I don't need this job, but I like getting out of the house and having something to do. That was the most embarrassing moment for me! Why are you stealing?"

"I'm so sorry, Mom. I don't know why. I guess for the thrill."

"Well, hopefully, a month-long grounding and loss of phone privileges will give you a hell of a thrill, because that's what's happening!"

I served out my sentence, and she never told my dad exactly why I was grounded. He would have lectured me for days, and she thought I had learned my lesson. She also admitted to me years later that she suspected I had stolen the blazer and blouse but didn't say it in the office. After the entire experience, I was officially scared straight and never, ever attempted shoplifting again.

Chapter 17
The Hospital

THE AMBULANCE WAS in the driveway when we arrived at her house. I ran to the front door and found Mom in the living room, on a tall stretcher with two paramedics getting her hooked up to oxygen and a heart monitor.

"Mom. Mom, can you hear me?" She opened her eyes when she heard my voice.

Winnie was hiding behind the chair in the corner and came darting toward me. I had a crazed Labradoodle jumping in my face, and she wouldn't calm down. I am sure she was traumatized by the paramedics and, most of all, Mom's condition. Mark grabbed Winnie by the collar and held her back.

Mom looked up from the oxygen mask but didn't say anything.

I was in shock and turned to the paramedic who seemed in charge and was on his cell talking to the hospital. "Hi, I'm her daughter; this is my husband. What's happening?"

"Are you the one who called for the ambulance?" he asked as he multitasked.

"Yes, yes, what is going on? Did she have another stroke?"

"I'm Jake Simons and we arrived about five minutes ago. The door was unlocked so we came in and found her unresponsive. Has your mom had a stroke recently?"

"Well, yes, sometime within the last year. They were mild, and they aren't exactly sure of the timeline. But nothing like this! Is she going to be OK?" I was desperately trying to maintain control and not be the whack job who falls apart under pressure. But I could feel my emotions taking over. Seeing her on that stretcher, wrapped in a blanket, already hooked to machines, and not moving a muscle, I was terrified.

Jake made eye contact with me and said calmly, "We're going to take her to Metro Hospital. Her pulse is weak, but she did wake up and tell us her name right before you arrived. Do you want to come in the ambulance and your husband can follow us?"

"Yes, of course," I said as I turned to Mark. He was nodding his head in agreement.

"Jule, grab her purse," he said. "You'll need her insurance information. I'll take Winnie to our house and meet you."

I don't remember much about the ride there except that Jake was talking to Mom in a loud voice, trying to get her to wake up, which she did a few times and then lost consciousness again. I know that she knew I was there because she looked right at me and I thought she might say something but didn't. I also remember watching the cars on the highway that didn't bother to pull off to the side of the road as the ambulance raced along with sirens and lights on. I was thinking, *what kind of asshole doesn't give a shit about whoever is in that emergency vehicle, possibly in a life-threatening situation?* I'm sure their need to get to work or breakfast or a dentist appointment was much more important. The sheer disregard and indifference for another person who was in trouble angered me, and I lost a little faith in humankind.

Four medical personnel were waiting in hospital scrubs and white coats when our ambulance arrived at the emergency entrance. Mom was rushed through the ER.

"You must be Suzanne's daughter? I'm the neurologist on duty, Dr. Wright. We understand that your mother has had strokes in the past, is that correct?"

"Yes, I think two or three mild ones in the last year. Is she OK?"

"We have initiated stroke alert protocol and are checking her out right now. Please wait here and someone will be out to speak to you as soon as we know more."

I stood in the hall trying to grasp any bit of information as people entered and exited the curtained room. Mark came in right after that, and I turned my attention to a welcomed face.

"What do they know so far? Any news?"

"Not really, but they're following stroke protocol since it seems the most likely situation. Oh, Mark. The ride here was awful. She was unconscious most of the trip and looked really bad. I'm fucking worried!"

"Let's see what they say and go from there, Jules."

Just then, a physician's assistant appeared from the room. "Hi, family, she has regained consciousness and we want to get her into a quick CT scan. We have administered some medications into her IV and she's responding, which is good. We'll have more news soon."

It's weird in those situations, but you only take in about a third of the information. They talk a lot and you just wait to grasp a few key words since your mind is in turmoil. Stroke. Conscious. CT scan. Back soon. And then they whisked her away. I tried to catch her eye, but everything was happening so fast, I missed her.

About 40 minutes later, they came back with a much smaller crew and Dr. Wright approached us. "OK, we've completed the CT scan and administered some stroke protocol drugs, and she is responding well. The CT scan did show a small brain bleed but not a stroke. This incident is potentially linked to the brain bleed, but it's small and shouldn't have had that effect. Currently, we need to check her into the hospital and perform some other tests to be sure."

"You just said not a stroke, correct? What are some of the other issues that could have caused this? You said a brain bleed?" My thoughts were jumbled, and I was grasping at straws.

"Yes, it was definitely not a stroke. We aren't sure of the exact cause. More tests will give us a better picture."

"Thank you, doctor, can we go in to see her?" Mark asked.

"Yes, she's awake and would like to see you guys. Please go ahead."

Then the doctor was gone, and the stroke team disbanded and moved to other areas of the hospital. We went in, and Mom was sitting up on the bed and sipping water from a straw.

"Mom, oh my God ... what the hell ... how are you doing?" I said all of this as I grabbed her in a tight hug.

"I really don't know what's happening, but they did say I'm not having another stroke." Her voice was hoarse, but I could make out the words. She sounded 100 percent better than she did on the phone call this morning. She even had a bright look in her eyes and some color in her face. This was not the same woman that I saw in the ambulance, unconscious and gray. I would not believe all of this had been on the same day if I hadn't experienced it myself. I was happy she was alert but confused by the events. I needed to call some people, like Kylie, my family, her siblings, Lorri, and Kent to update them, but I had no idea what to say at this point.

She was moved to a nice private room on the eighth floor. Fully alert and somewhat bitchy, she started to complain.

"I really feel better now and would like to go home. They can't really keep me here as a hostage, can they? Hospitals aren't the best place to be if you want to feel better."

"I think you're being a tad bit hasty, Mom. You were in an ambulance and unconscious a few hours ago."

"Why the hell is all of this happening to me? I can't really remember much from last night up until a few hours ago. Julie, what do you know about all of this? Tell me now!"

So, I told her about the phone calls this morning and what she said, and Jake, the EMT, and how we ended up in the ambulance. I also recapped the time in the emergency room. She didn't remember any of it. I was starting to think that maybe we were entering the world of dementia or Alzheimer's. Any explanation at this point would have been welcome because the unknown was extremely frightening.

I called my siblings from the hallway while Mom was sleeping. Not having a diagnosis to give them made it seem less urgent, but I think they could tell by my tone how concerned I was. They sprung into action and Jeff was the first to arrive.

"Things are not looking good, Jeff. Once we got the stroke diagnosis from the neurologist, I thought she would be on the road to some improvement. But she's just getting worse. The CT scan from this morning showed no strokes but some sort of small brain bleed, and they really don't know what the fuck is happening. We may need to go to the University of Michigan or Cleveland Clinic. What do you think?"

Jeff was a University of Michigan graduate and knew they had an amazing medical facility. "Yes, I feel like U of M may be the next step. You may not notice since you see her every day, but she looks a lot worse than when I saw her at Christmas. It's kind of alarming, and she has lost a lot more weight."

"Really, Jeff? You think I don't notice? I *do* notice, and it scares the shit out of me." I was tearing up and felt I was being judged. "I've tried to get her to put weight on, but it hasn't been working. I know it's bad, and she isn't getting any better! I just don't know what to do!"

"Hey, hey, Sis. It's not your fault. We'll figure this out," Jeff said as he pulled me into a hug. I stayed there for a minute, took some deep breaths, then pulled away and calmed down.

"They're doing a round of tests tomorrow and then I think we should decide from there. I'll probably need to call her primary to get a referral for a U of M neurologist. If they don't have any other ideas, I say we get her out of here. Let's just see what happens tomorrow," I said. Jeff agreed.

Jon and Jen arrived later that night, and Kent and Lorri both called. I also heard from my Uncle James and Aunt Karen. Everyone was asking a lot of questions, and my answers seemed lame. I felt like an inadequate advocate. But my thoughts were only focused on my mom. She looked much weaker in that hospital bed. The machines were inanimate sentinels with rhythmic blinking and beeping that might keep her from sleeping. My sister and I asked the nurse on duty about staying over that night, and she suggested we let Mom rest, as they would be giving her a sleeping aid.

We didn't want to leave her there with so much unanswered. The situation was spinning out of control and I had no idea what the next day or even the next hour would bring. I had the urge to connect with her somehow, to let her know she was not alone. She was in a deep, drug-induced sleep, so it seemed that she was in capable hands. We kissed her and left for the night.

Chapter 18
The Family Room

THE NEXT DAY STARTED off well enough with coffee and smart remarks around my kitchen island. I loved having my family around even if it was impossible to forget the stressful circumstances. There was a lot of discussion about the previous day's events and speculation about what was happening.

"I just can't get my head around the total of these symptoms. There has to be a common denominator that ties them together," Jon pondered aloud.

"I hate to bring it up, but am I the only one who thinks this could be related to a brain tumor, like Aunt Kink?" Jeff threw it out there and then was quiet.

"Yeah, Mom has brought that up herself, but with Aunt Kink, there were severe headaches and blurred vision. She's had none of that. Plus, that would have shown up on a previous scan," I added while I rustled through the fridge for raspberry jam.

"Maybe a neurological disorder like Parkinson's disease, or even something like MS. I have a friend whose mom has MS, and there are some common symptoms. Hopefully today we will learn something!" Jenny added.

We headed to the hospital in two cars. Jen and Mark hopped in with me as I drove and talked with Kylie on speakerphone.

"I just don't understand why they still don't know what's wrong with Grandma. I thought you said she had some small strokes and that's why she was swallowing weird and walking a little unstably. Didn't you say that, Mom?" Kylie seemed frustrated just like the rest of us.

"Yes, that's what the neurologist told us from her last CT scan. But now, they don't think that's what happened. They just don't know. It sounds ridiculous, but I am at a loss, too!"

Jen added, "Some of these medical people are idiots. They don't have a clue what's going on!"

That only fueled Ky more. "Mom, we have to get her somewhere else so she can get some real help!"

"I know, Kylie. We're letting them finish the round of tests today, and then we're going to make a plan. We've discussed other hospitals and I've been looking into other doctors. Who knows? Moving her too soon could also be a mistake. Right now, she needs some hydration and she's also seeing the dietician about the weight-loss issues. Let's see what we can find out today."

Again, feeling like an inadequate piece of shit, I hung up with Ky. I promised to fill her in later that day. At most times in my life, I have been good at planning, overcoming obstacles, and working out a solution. I was trying to stay positive and be the voice of reason but felt like I was failing Mom. This frustration was like stale bile in the back of my throat. There was an empty nagging in my core that made me want to cry and wretch at the same time. Since I couldn't do either, I had to hold it together.

When I arrived at the hospital room, Jeff and Jon were standing by the window with stunned looks on their faces. I thought Mom was sleeping, but she was so still and rigid that I couldn't be sure. Her frail body was like a small child swallowed up by that big hospital bed. There were lots of cords and equipment dangling next to her. She wasn't hooked up to anything except an IV, but I noticed the cords from the beeping medical devices hanging beside her bed intertwined like a pit of vipers in different shades of beige. That was a perfect metaphor for the inconclusive diagnosis we had received—slippery, elusive, and unpredictable.

Her head was tilted almost too far back on the pillow, and her mouth was wide open in a slack position. She had some drool coming out of the side and her lips were milky pale. Her face was a whitewashed peach/gray, and her breathing was so shallow and slight that I was instantly alarmed. I had never seen her like that before, even when I had peeked in on her during a nap. Now, I wanted to wake her just to make sure that she was alive and all right. Just then, a nurse breezed into the room already talking.

"Good morning, are you Suzanne's family?" She wrote her name on the dry erase board that had sections for information like attending physician, day nurse, special diet information, and family names. I read the word "Janice" on the board as she continued talking very quickly but easily and friendly, which lightened the mood in the room. After focusing on her words, we nodded in unison. I was still taken aback by what was going on.

"Suzanne was extremely tired because we had her in tests until about four hours ago. We gave her a mild sedative so she can rest comfortably. Why don't we step into the family room two doors down on the right and I can bring you up to speed on the results so far?"

The room felt surprisingly welcoming, and the two sofas and four chairs were basic but comfortable. The geometric design on the carpet screamed commercial grade, but somehow it was relaxing. There was also a television, coffee bar, and vending machines; one for snacks and another for soda and water. There was a small refrigerator, an array of magazines, a few paperback books, and some popular board games stacked on a shelf. I momentarily imagined fathers and mothers and siblings huddled together in cautious anticipation as a doctor stood before them ready to deliver news of their loved one. My palms were sweating as I anticipated what was to come. I was careful to remain optimistic even though it was difficult.

"Are you all children of Suzanne's?" Janice asked after she got settled in one of the chairs.

Jeff responded, "Yes, we're all of her children. We came in last night except for my sister, Julie, who lives in the area."

"OK. Julie, you were with her when she came in, correct?" She was now looking at the laptop chart.

I nodded, still not finding my words, and unable to shake my mom's frail appearance. I knew that there would be many of the same questions that I had answered dozens of times, so I tried to find my voice. But she didn't start with questions.

"This morning she had blood tests, a urine analysis, a chest X-ray, an EKG, two CT scans, and an MRI," Janice read from the laptop. "Although you will get to see her attending physician on rounds in about an hour, I can tell you that nothing significant has been found. Her levels are normal, and it looks like she may have a UTI, so we are administering an antibiotic, but nothing else so far."

We took in that information and I locked eyes with Jenny. She had small tears, I assumed from relief, but she didn't say a word.

"So, we don't know what caused the episode that got her here yesterday?" I asked.

"And what about all of this information about strokes that we have been given? Is that not true?" Jon asked.

"Also, the weight loss and the unsteadiness, and all of the other symptoms. What is going on?" Jeff escalated his voice on this last part, but Janice remained calm.

"Look, I know this is good news but still doesn't answer all of these questions. Dr. Ray from neurology has been consulted, and she will be looking at the case and all the test information to give you her analysis. Also, the attending physician will be around shortly, and I will tell him that you'd like to talk."

She closed the laptop, gave a pleasant smile, and left the room. I wasn't mad at her, simply confused and bewildered. I am sure that Janice had encountered this before, and it was just part of the job.

"What the fuck?!" Jon said once she was out of earshot.

"Exactly. Mom looks like complete hell and there are no answers." Jen was visibly annoyed.

"I know, guys, this is a fuckshow. I'm so sorry that we don't know anything more than we did since this all started, but at least she's in the hospital now and maybe we'll get some answers." I tried to bring the room back to some reality. They hadn't seen her since Christmas, and I knew it was a shock. Over the next hour, we alternated between making phone calls and checking in the room to see if she was awake yet. It was Saturday, but Jeff and Jon were also scheduling with their jobs to stay over through the start of the week. Once everyone was back in the family room, I took the opportunity to pull us together.

"Hey, I understand that we all have obligations, but I'm hoping we can make some decisions as a family. She's not able to stay at her house, and I have been arguing with her for the past few weeks but she still won't take my offer to stay with us. She's been there for the weekends but then wants to go back home. She needs more supervision, so we should talk about that as well."

"Maybe once we have a little more data, we can see if there's a way to keep her in her house with a nurse to check on her, or one of those alert systems." Jeff was always the optimist.

"It would help if someone could tell us what in the hell is causing all of this so we can make some solid decisions!" Jenny repeated.

"You're right, Sis. Let's see what the next few days bring, but I need your help figuring this out."

They agreed, and we hoped to make some decisions and devise a new plan. The attending physician soon appeared at the door of the family room, introduced himself, and shook our hands. He looked about thirty-five years old, was tall, and wore glasses. He had a great bedside manner and put us at ease right away.

"Janice filled me in on some of your questions, and I can't blame you. You'll probably have even more because there aren't a lot of answers at this point. Your mother is sick, and we are determined to find out what is causing her symptoms. Tests did uncover a blood clot on her brain. It's not large and is probably due to a fall. Has she been falling a lot?"

"I know about three times. Most recently on Thursday night. There could be others since she doesn't always tell me everything," I said.

"Blood clots are usually from head trauma, and that's what it looks like. It doesn't explain her long-term symptoms like the weight loss, but it's something that we found. She has lost a considerable amount of weight in the past few months, so a dietician will be by today to talk to you. Also, the neurology department is looking over all the tests and will be sending Dr. Ray to see her as well. What else can I answer right now?"

"Doctor, we were told that she had been having small strokes and that's what was causing her swallowing and balance problems. Is that not the case?" I asked.

"Well, as I mentioned, we saw a blood clot, but that isn't the cause of the long-term issues. I'm going to stop in the room now and see if I can examine her."

Basically, without throwing another doctor under the bus, he just admitted the stroke idea was a bunch of bullshit. We thought about that as he wrapped up and went to see Mom. When he finished, she was awake and happy to see us all.

"Well, I must really be in trouble if you're all here. Remember, on my tombstone, I want it to read, 'I told you I was sick,'" she said with slurred speech and a raspy cough, but it was good to see her back to her sassy self.

"Yeah, Mom, we probably won't do that, but keep thinking of suggestions," Jon teased her as he went in for a cheek kiss.

"Oh, Mom, how are you doing? We are so worried," Jen said, wiping her eyes.

"I just don't know what the hell is going on with me," she said as her voice cracked.

"That's what we're here to find out, Mom. Don't worry." Jeff was always to the point.

There was a light knock on the door and a woman came in with some flowers. It was a vase of big white lilies and roses with other greenery, purple statice, and baby's breath. There was a card on a post in the arrangement that read *Thank you for being the best grandmother anyone could ask for. We all love you very much. Stay strong, sending endless love.* And it was signed by all the grandchildren. It had Kylie's fingerprints all over it and was exactly what my mom needed. She read the card and then passed it around. The smile made her color much better, and the room was immediately brighter.

"That is so sweet. They know I love fresh flowers. They smell amazing." She held them to her nose, closed her eyes, and smiled. Flowers always had a way of calming her down. It was her best sedative.

The hospital dietician came by in the afternoon to talk about her diet. Jen and I were also in the room. Jeff and Jon had gone to a late lunch: we were dining in shifts so that someone was always there. She went through a lot of questions with Mom about what she had been able to eat. After listening intently, she said Mom would need about 1800 calories a day to stop the weight loss. She went through some menu ideas and the total calorie counts. She recommended soft meals and gave my sister some suggestions. Drinking Ensure between meals could help boost the calories as well. I knew Mom was getting overwhelmed by all this; she hadn't been able to eat even half the amount that the dietician was suggesting.

"That's a lot of food for her, and she has trouble swallowing even half of what you're talking about," I said. I felt like I needed to verbalize what Mom was probably thinking.

The dietician stopped talking and paused. "Well then, you need to find ways to pack volume. For example, if you have one drink, add as many calories to it as you can. Like Ensure plus ice cream plus a protein mix and maybe chocolate sauce or fruit. Make a thin shake and then she can get a good number of extra calories in one drink."

I could see Mom lighten a little. "That even sounds good to me," she cracked.

The dietician then broke the momentary good mood with, "Otherwise, we will need a feeding tube to get basic nutrition." She looked at me when she said it, and I knew what she meant. If my mom couldn't start eating a lot more than she had been, this would be the next step. Jen didn't say a word and Mom didn't, either. The last time we had this come up, Mom had been much healthier, so we didn't get so offended this time. We wrapped it up with a few more questions and she promised to stop by with specific diet plans before my mom was discharged.

Dr. Ray from neurology also came in later that day to introduce herself. She was of Indian descent and had long dark hair up in a loose bun. She wore a little lipstick and small pearl earrings. The accent was thick, but we could understand her until she began discussing medical information. She was friendly but not overly so. It was obvious she had at least looked over Mom's chart. She wanted to come back tomorrow at 11:00 a.m. for a follow-up exam. "I think someone should be here. Is that possible?"

"Yes, we will be here."

Chapter 19
The Heartbreak

WE STAYED AT THE HOSPITAL until Mom fell into a deep sleep. Everyone headed back to my house and ate a dinner that Mark pulled together while we recapped the day. Jeff and Jon had checked into my mom's insurance just to make sure all was well with her healthcare coverage. They had also taken time to research a few new doctor options at the University of Michigan and Cleveland Clinic. The men seemed much more comfortable digging into the tangible items while we wrestled with the messier abstract issues. I scrolled through my phone and noticed that there were some voicemails that I needed to return. My mom's siblings were due an update and so was Kylie, who had called me four times. Kent wanted to come by the hospital the next day, and I knew Mom wouldn't want him there while she was in that state, so I needed to talk to him.

After an hour of dividing these calls with my sister, I finally started to listen to the other voicemails. There was one from IdeaLab in Detroit.

"Hi Julie, it's Ron Carson from IdeaLab. I'm sorry I missed you because I have some news regarding your app, Friendly Neighbors. Please give me a call back when you get this message. Thanks, and talk soon."

I really wasn't prepared to think about business, and it was late, but I called him back anyway.

"Hi Julie, so glad you called. I have an investor who is interested in your mobile app. They're anxious to have a discussion in person in the coming week. Is that something we could set up?"

I had actually forgotten about the presentation and the hunt for investors. None of that really seemed to matter right now, but I feigned enthusiasm. "Oh wow, that's fantastic. I have some family issues right now, but I will figure out a plan for a meeting. Can I get back to you in the next few days?"

"Oh yes. Hope everything is OK. Just let me know what might work since it's best to strike while the iron is hot, so to speak."

"Of course, I'll get right back. Thanks so much, Ron."

There was no way I could make a meeting with everything going on in my family. I decided that I would wait until morning to talk to Mark because he was already asleep, and then call Oliver. I was exhausted, and it was too late to do anything tonight.

I slept like a rock, which was surprising considering there was so much on my mind. I woke up early to hot breath about four inches from my face. I slowly opened my eyes and there was Winnie at the side of my bed, panting and whining and holding a pink stuffed monkey in her mouth. Her eyelashes looked a foot long and her big brown eyes were searching for answers. I know she missed my mom. It was hard to tell what was going through her cute little dog brain, but she clearly needed some attention. Her innocence helped me to find a new perspective from the heaviness of my thoughts. It would be refreshing to spend some time with her.

I got up, put on some yoga pants and a pullover, and we went for a walk through the hills of the neighborhood. It was so quiet at 6:00 a.m., long before cars headed off to church or breakfast on this crisp Sunday morning. Pinecones and needles crackled under our steps and the air was still. Rabbits, squirrels, and chipmunks scampered through the fallen trees and leafy branches. Winnie just kept walking straight ahead, so content to be out in the fresh air. It was a perfect calm setting to organize my thoughts for the day. I decided to have a discussion with Mark about the new developments with Friendly Neighbors. I hoped that he could go to a meeting with Oliver in tow to talk to the potential investors. Mark was great with business plans and financial deals. Oliver knew the product inside and out and would be a great sidekick.

Mark was up when I returned from the relaxing walk, and he gave me a big hug as I told him about the call from Ron Carson. "Jules, this is great news! I knew you would get some interest. So proud of you!"

"Well, let's see how excited you are when I ask you a big f'ing favor, mister. They want to have a meeting next week in Detroit. There's no way I can make that happen with all that's going on with Mom. Do you think you could go with Oliver and get the preliminaries on the investment option for me?" I used my best sultry stare, stopped talking, and crossed my fingers. In a negotiation, the first one to speak loses.

Mark finally answered, "The beginning of the week will be hard, but let's see what we can set up. Thursday or Friday would be best. If that can work, I'd be happy to help you out with this." He gave me a sweet smile, and I jumped up to hug him.

"You're the best. I'll make some calls today on the way to the hospital." I gave him a kiss and started pulling out bagels and cream cheese for the breakfast crowd that would emerge from guest rooms at any moment.

Soon, I was on my way to the hospital and made a call to Oliver to share the news.

"That's amazing news! Did he mention the investment group's name? I might know them."

"No, he didn't, but I'm going to call him next and get more information. Do you think you could go to a meeting later this week with Mark and the investors? My mom's in the hospital and I don't think that I'll be able to attend, but Mark plans to go on the business side for us."

"Oh no, that's bad news. Is she going to be alright?" Oliver asked.

"We really don't know what's going on yet. They're running tests."

"Well, I'm sending good thoughts, Jules, and absolutely, I'm down for a trip into the 'D' with Mark." He interrupted me as I started giving rough details, "Just let me know the details when you get them," Oliver said.

I hung up and called Ron Carson. He rattled off a lot of information, and I didn't write any of it down since I was in the car, but he planned to set something up for Thursday afternoon. I told him about my mom and that I would not be able to come that Thursday, and he was very sympathetic. I gave him Mark's cell phone instead to confirm the details. It all seemed under control, and I mentally checked it off my list.

We all arrived at the hospital around 9:30 a.m. to find Mom awake and staring at a tray that was sitting on her bed table. It was breakfast, and she hadn't touched a thing. She was looking at it like it was an alien.

"Hi, Mom. You look much better today. How did you sleep?" We started to make small talk with her and tried to cheer her up. It was obvious that she was cranky and exhausted.

"They don't really let you sleep around here. Which is funny since you're in the hospital and they keep wanting you to rest. But then they bang around all night and come in and check on you every twenty minutes, so there's no way in hell to get any rest." She ran out of air at the end of the rant and there were some expletives, but they were under her breath.

"Yeah, that doesn't make much sense, Mom. Sorry you're still tired," Jen said.

"Have you seen any doctors this morning?" Jon asked.

"No. A few nurses checked on me and delivered this tray of mystery food. I guess it's breakfast," she said, motioning to the tray.

It had many little containers, and when I looked closer, it was all soft food. Possibly some tapioca pudding and some whipped fruit with cream cheese maybe... none of it was easily recognizable.

"Can you just try to eat some of it, Mom?" Jenny asked.

"I will if you will," she slurred with an abundance of saliva.

We took her challenge literally and each of us grabbed a container and a spoon to test the flavors. We made sure she took bites as well. Identifying the food was tough, but we were up for the challenge. There were some big laughs and sour faces as we tried to pin down the origins of the inedible concoctions. It was good to see Mom laugh, which was probably the best thing we could do for her at that point.

Jeff and Jon left the room around 10:30 to make some quick work-related phone calls. Dr. Ray sauntered in just before 11:00 a.m. and had two younger residents from neurology with her. My brothers weren't back yet, but it was probably for the best because we now had six people in that small hospital room, and it was a bit crowded. We made introductions and she turned toward my mom and reached for her hand.

"Hello, Suzanne. How are you doing today?"

"I guess better than when I arrived but still feeling very tired and weak. Not great," she responded, but struggled to enunciate.

"I would like to give you a short examination if that's OK with you." Dr. Ray paused, and my mom nodded her approval.

"Can you open your mouth and stick out your tongue? Can you say ahh and ooh, again, please? Suzanne, do you ever experience weakness in your mouth and tongue?"

"Yes, I notice my throat feeling numb, and I have trouble swallowing. Sometimes I get a sensation that my tongue feels a little heavier. I've been told that my speech sounds slurred sometimes, and some people have even said they thought I sounded drunk."

I knew she was referring to her sister, Lois, who had called me a few weeks ago concerned that my mom might be drinking heavily. I made sure she knew that wasn't the case, but it didn't stop her suspicions. My mom was very hurt by this because my aunt mentioned it to other family members, who also called to check on her.

Dr. Ray tested her reflexes. She measured her ability to push with her arms and legs. I had seen those tests before in her regular exams with Dr. Krill. Mom always seemed to have good strength when doing those exercises. Then Dr. Ray examined her back with her gown open. This went on for a few minutes and Jenny and I looked at each other, questioning the significance. She called the residents over, and they looked as well.

This went on for a few minutes until finally my mom shifted her shoulders and said, "OK, what the hell are you looking at back there?"

Dr. Ray apologized and closed the gown. The residents moved back to their corner of the room. She turned my mom back to a sitting position against the bed. "I was looking at your back and shoulder muscles. I noticed some small fasciculations or twitches. Do you ever feel these twitches in your muscles, Suzanne?"

"Maybe a little, and I do notice numbness sometimes." She said it so innocently that it seemed unimportant, but the doctors looked at each other.

Just then, Jeff and Jon came into the crowded room. Dr. Ray introduced herself and turned quickly back to my mom. She took a deep breath, and they locked eyes. Then she said slowly and very clearly, "I believe you have Amyotrophic Lateral Sclerosis or ALS. This is a progressive neurodegenerative disease that affects nerve cells in the brain and spinal cord." She stopped there and put her hand on my mom's shoulder.

They say you can hear a pin drop when a room becomes extremely quiet. That was not the pristine quiet that I experienced. I could hear my blood flow constrict in my throat and my pulse pounding faster and faster under my skin. I could hear my mom's chest heave as her brain twisted and seized with confusion at what she had just heard. My sister gasped, and my brothers shifted their weight back and forth nervously. I could hear too many things in that quiet room.

Dr. Ray continued, "Everything that I've looked at in your tests, and during this exam, suggests this is the conclusion. We can't be sure until we administer a test called an EMG and a nerve conduction study. We have our head of neurology, Dr. Merrill, who is also an ALS specialist, scheduled to come by later today to see you. His office does the testing outside of the hospital."

We all remained still and silent. I fixed my eyes on one of the residents in the corner while I tried to focus my thoughts. She was a woman in her mid-thirties, and I saw that she had glistening tears in her eyes that were sparkling from the hospital lights. She tried to turn away so I couldn't see, but it was too late. For some reason, that moment was the catalyst that sprung me off that tiny sofa and over to the bed.

My mom was unusually quiet, her eyes searching. She seemed to be struggling to understand the doctor's prognosis. I put my arm around her, and she whispered to me, "Is that Lou Gehrig's disease she's talking about? Is that the same thing? That's really bad."

The news hung thick in the air, the silence broken as Jen and I sobbed openly. Jeff and Jon moved to the bed and we were in a completely shambled and trembling group hug. We didn't know a lot about this particularly evil disease, but we knew there was no current cure.

"Let's find out for sure before we jump to conclusions," Jeff mumbled as we all held tight.

"Can we get this Dr. Merrill's contact information please?" Jon turned to Dr. Ray.

"Yes, of course. He'll be in the hospital this evening, and I know he wants to speak to Suzanne and all of you," she said and handed over a card.

We needed time to be alone and to process the explosion of information that she had just detonated.

"I am so sorry. Is there anything that I can answer for you right at this minute?"

No one said a word, and she and her team reluctantly turned toward the door. Just like that, lives had been altered, our hopes smashed. That moment was now indelibly etched in my brain to replay over and over. As doctors shuffled quietly out the door, the young female resident glanced back over her shoulder, and her expression sent a shiver down my spine.

Chapter 20
The Next

WE MET WITH DR. MERRILL, and I was taken with how he held my mom's hand while he spoke to her. Based on our combined research, we found him to be a highly rated ALS specialist but also someone demonstrating immense compassion. He and his team spent their days working with ALS patients in an office in a new medical facility about one mile from my neighborhood. There was no way that a person could devote their life to the care of terminally ill people without a special purpose to provide comfort and peace in their darkest time. Later that day, he talked to us for hours and held my mom's hand and looked her directly in the eyes. He even hugged her as she cried. Although there was a test to administer, he felt confident that this was ALS. She had all the symptoms, and he also estimated she was in her second or third year of the disease.

So many thoughts went through my head. *How was this happening? Why her? What will we do to move forward?* The next few days were a blur, but we did move forward by getting Mom discharged and settled in at my house. There were no discussions about her going back home at that point; she accepted that she would need help. We would be forced to look into the future soon and decide on a course of action but for now, we were just taking it day by day.

Moving into a highly organized mode, we made numerous phone calls and tried to stay on topic, but they all went something like this: "Mom is out of the hospital and has been diagnosed with ALS. There is one last test later this week for a final confirmation. We are still hoping this is not the case, but all her symptoms are pointing to ALS. She is feeling better right now and will be temporarily staying at Julie's house. She isn't ready for calls yet, but hopefully soon. We will let her know that you're sending love and prayers."

Those calls were incredibly painful as they were to her brothers and sisters, Kent, Lorri, and a few other close friends and family who had been checking in. The most difficult call was to Kylie. She sobbed and went silent before asking the often-unaskable question: "How much time does she have?"

I told her the truth: "No one really knows."

Learning about ALS became my primary focus. It was my new obsession, and I was determined to arm myself with all the facts. It helped to distract me but as I dug deeper, it also scared me to my core. Through my research, I learned that ALS is an insidious monster that doesn't provide a road map of the devastation to come. It is different for everyone, and there is no identical version. My mom's symptoms indicated bulbar ALS, which is why her throat and tongue were the first main areas to be affected. The nerves to these muscles were not getting signals from the brain, which affects speech and swallowing and would eventually stop her from breathing as well. I knew this because I had started diving into information on the internet. I learned many things I did not want to know and stalled my research to avoid becoming too depressed.

When Mom wasn't resting or staring out the window, she had long phone calls with Kylie. Their bond seemed to grow stronger each day, and they leaned on each other for strength. They talked for long stretches, and I even heard Mom laughing a few times.

Thursday was an important day at our house. Not only was Mom scheduled for the EMG test, but Mark was prepping for the

IdeaLab meeting in Detroit. My brothers had returned to their homes but promised to come back on the weekend, so that left me and my sister to navigate the medical maze ahead of us. We gathered around the breakfast table to plan our day.

"I have no idea what to wear to this thing," Mom said as she shuffled into the kitchen. She had slowed down since the hospital. Most of the time, I helped her walk by taking her arm. It can't be easy to deal with the knowledge that you most likely have a terminal illness that is chipping away at your body. The mental gravity of the situation was draining and quickly taking its physical toll.

"Probably just be comfortable, Mom. They said it could take over an hour," Jen responded.

I made her a shake in the blender with vanilla Ensure, ice cream, and strawberry sauce. She had drunk that same concoction the day before and seemed to like it, so I tried it again.

"So, Julie, is this all I am ever going to get in the morning now? You found one thing that I actually finished, and that's my only choice?" she asked and laughed.

I wished I could bottle that laugh and listen to it over and over. It was such a common occurrence in the past that I hadn't fully appreciated it . Now, I couldn't get enough.

"You know I am a sucky cook, Mom. This could be it."

She winked at me and took a good-natured swig.

Mark had a few questions for me about the business plan for Friendly Neighbors. "My tactic will be to get the information, negotiate any rough edges and leave the final decision to you once we have all of the details. Does that sound like a good approach for today?"

I couldn't have cared less about any of it right then but tried to stay enthusiastic. My perspective had completely shifted, and it just didn't seem to matter. "Honestly, I really appreciate you guys going but don't have any expectations for the outcome. I just can't focus right now, so please do whatever makes sense at the moment. I trust you."

"Jules, just take a breath. We'll get through all of this, you'll see." Then he kissed me, hugged Mom, and headed out the door.

Dr. Merrill's office was less than five minutes from my house. The EMG was performed by a young physician on Dr. Merrill's team. The test involved several painful pricks in her muscles and then a process that measured her strength. Apparently, it was the only way to detect ALS. After she suffered through the test, we went to a comfortable office to talk to Dr. Merrill.

"I have been over the results of the nerve conduction study and the EMG. The muscles are not responding correctly to your nerve signals, and this suggests a progressive nerve disorder. That, coupled with all your other test results, tells us definitively that you do have ALS. I am so sorry, Suzanne. Also, I think you may be a bit further along in the disease than originally predicted since your breathing is also weakened."

We all sat still, reeling from the continued gut punches.

"What are the next steps? What can we do to combat the progression?" Jen asked.

"I know this is a lot to process, but I strongly recommend our assistance clinics for ALS patients. These are facilitated every Tuesday here at my office to teach ways to stay mobile for as long as possible before the body loses its abilities. Studies have shown that patients who attend the clinics have better symptom management, maintain as much independence as possible, and have an improved quality of life."

I looked at my mom, and her face was expressionless. While I stared at her, I could still hear him talking in the background, but it sounded like far away gibberish.

"There is also a good amount of equipment that she will need: a hospital bed, a BiPap breathing machine, a cough-assist device, a portable toilet chair, a walker, a wheelchair, and a ramp into the house. I will prescribe all the needed items and get them delivered promptly. Another immediate consideration will be the feeding tube. It is often essential for continued dietary needs and eventually for administering medication. It would be good to think about that now since your breathing is already compromised and will limit surgical options later on."

I sat there listening to Dr. Merrill while I held my mom's hand and thought, *is it possible to resume life after days like this one?* The information seemed so clinical, and I had no idea what we were facing. But I knew one thing that hung over all the discussions: My mom was going to die from ALS, and there wasn't a damn thing we could do to stop it. Our only hope, however remote, was to slow it down.

Mark called after we returned home. He was still on the road from Detroit. Mom had wanted to lie down, so I set her up in the guest room we had prepared. She was out before I even left the room.

"Julie, how did it go today?"

"As bad as possible. They confirmed the diagnosis, and it's definitely ALS."

"Oh no. God damn it. I'm so sorry. How is she doing?"

"She seems numb, like she's not really taking in what they're saying. I totally understand since I'm in overload myself. It's just too much to process. They're sending some deliveries in the next few days, lots of things she'll need like a hospital bed, walker, and eventually a wheelchair. I'm so scared and worried for her, Mark. I just don't know what to do." I started to cry. It was a release from the day that I couldn't stop.

"Hey, Jules, Jules, take a breath. It's OK. I wanted to talk to you this morning, but there was so much going on today. I think we should just have her move in with us permanently if that's what you want to do. We can take care of her and get some help when we need it. What do you think?"

There have been so many days where I have looked at this man and felt a deep gratitude that I found this kind of love. Those were the sweet, quiet moments where you just know that you are in the exact right place with the right person. Still, that couldn't compare to the love I felt hearing him say this one sentence that made me feel some control when things were spinning so crazily out of control. It took me a few seconds to get the words out since I was so emotional. "Yes, I hoped you would say that. I don't want to have her anywhere else."

"OK, then we'll figure it out and make it work. But there's one big issue we need to consider," Mark added.

"There are probably a million issues we need to consider, but what's the one you are talking about?"

"It's totally understandable but you haven't even asked how the meeting went this morning at IdeaLab," he said.

"Oh, yeah, that. I guess I forgot. What happened?"

"Well, it went great, and you have a group that is interested in fully financing your prototype including the testing period, product development, and marketing. They like the overall idea and have offered a substantial investment and full team support. It all sounds great except that they want full control of the direction of the product."

"What do you mean? They want to just buy it from us outright? Take over?" I sputtered. It was nice to relieve my pent-up frustration and hostility at a deserved target.

"Well, we can be involved, but they will have the final say on everything related to the product. And I'm not sure they are as keenly focused on helping seniors as the original concept is geared."

"That's probably a deal-breaker for me since that's the demographic," I said.

"Yes, Julie, I know how you feel. We'll need to discuss it from the business side and try to take emotion out of it."

"Taking emotion out of anything is not my strong suit these days. And I really don't care right now. I guess we can discuss it more later. Please drive safely, and I'll see you when you get here."

I peeked into the door of the room that we now called my mom's room. She was sound asleep and snoring lightly. Winnie was lying at the bottom of her bed, and she lifted her head to monitor the door. My sister came up behind me and touched my arm. We backed out into the master bedroom next door, and I told her what Mark and I had decided about moving her in permanently.

"Oh God, Julie, do you really mean it? She's going to need a lot of care, and it's going to be hard. I don't think you know what all is going to happen."

"Of course, I don't. None of us do, but I want her here. Dr. Merrill suggested getting in touch with Visiting Nurses to get some help a few times a week. I can do that when the time comes. I need her to feel support and love and not to go through this alone. I know you'll help when you can. Mark is on board, so we're going to do it."

"Of course, I'll help as much as I can, Julie. Let me go call the boys so we can start figuring out a plan to move her in and get her organized with what she'll need here."

It was a relief to at least have a plan.

Chapter 21
The Move

I WAS GOING THROUGH the motions of trying to prepare dinner. I really didn't give a damn what we had to eat, but it was a good diversion from all the conversations screaming in my head. Was I crazy to think I could care for her on my own? How bad would it get? Would it be better for her to have professional care? How ridiculous was it that this investor has decided I couldn't have a say in my own product? What the hell was I going to make that Mom would eat?

As I was absorbed in my conflicted inner dialogue, I turned from the pantry and Mom was standing by the island staring at my back. "Oh my gosh, Mom, I didn't know you were up from your nap."

"I didn't want to sleep too long and decided I should get up. I had a whacky dream about civil war soldiers. They were in your woods out back in tattered uniforms trying to decide how to get some water because they were very thirsty. One of them had been wounded but seemed OK and was very focused on water. They had an old silver cup that retracted into itself and became small just like the one my dad had. Do you remember that cup?"

"That's kind of a strange dream, but yes, I do remember it. It was from your great-grandfather, I think."

"Yeah, I had forgotten about it, but I need to find that cup. I just remembered it, and I want to see it. Can you help me look for it when we go back to my house?"

This dream seemed odd, and maybe there was a deeper meaning related to how she was feeling: lost, scared, hopeless ... this was something I should try to figure out but more importantly, I realized that I had not talked to her about staying with us. I suddenly felt nervous since I didn't know if she would be open to the idea. She hadn't been a fan of the concept the last time I suggested it.

"Mom, do you want something to drink? That dream probably made *you* thirsty. Maybe some tea?"

She nodded her approval and shuffled over to the table to sit down. I put on the kettle and joined her. I reached out for her hand and said very casually, "How are you feeling? Better after the nap?" I didn't want to get too deep into the rest. I was sure she was still processing all the information just like me.

"Better but realized as soon as I woke up—it hit me right in the stomach—that I am totally fucked. I had hoped that there was another possibility, a miracle, who knows. Hoping despite everything that I don't have ALS, but that's just not the case. I feel hopeless, Julie."

I was surprised at her strong language and that she wanted to jump right into the subject. I squeezed her hand and looked her in the eyes. This was my chance. "Mom, you know we're not going to let you deal with this alone. I want you to move in here permanently. I promise to do everything in my power to be by your side every step of the way. I know that's not much, but I hope it makes you feel supported."

"I can't do that. I had a friend at work years ago whose husband had ALS. It was terrible every day for them. This thing is going to suck the life out of me, and I can't have you and Mark suffering, too. I think we should look at some other options."

She was being brave, but I saw the heartbreaking lost look in her eyes. "Hell, no. There are no other options. You're staying here. Jenny is going to help as much as she can. Jeff and Jon are coming back into town tomorrow afternoon, and we're going to take you over to the house to get the things that you want right now. Plus, Mom, Winnie needs to be with you, and she's comfortable here."

"Oh, Julie, you have no idea what you're saying. This is going to get hard." She began to cry, and so did I. "What did Mark say?"

"He's completely on board. It was his idea, and we can get help if we need it. It will work out, you'll see."

She looked at me for a long moment. "Let's give it a try and see how it goes, Julie. Who knows, you might drive ME crazy. You know you can be bitchy and bossy. A real Bitch-Boss."

"Well, I come by the first part naturally. It's in the genes." We both laughed and wiped our tears.

Over the next few days, we had a hospital bed delivered and various other equipment arrived as well. The guys took a few loads from her house and Jen and I set up her room. There was a low plant stand at the window, and she chose eight plants of various sizes. There was also a stained-glass terrarium full of more plants that lit up and cast colored lighting from the stained glass. We left the remaining plants in her house for now. We already had the beginnings of an entire ecosystem in her new bedroom. I wasn't sure how I would keep the plants alive with my black thumb, but I could give it a shot.

We had her tall dresser brought in and covered the top with framed photos. She wanted her own bedding even though it didn't fit on the small hospital bed, but we folded and draped until it worked. We also put a dog bed in the corner for Winnie and filled the closet with her clothes. My mom had always been the best-dressed woman in the room and spent most of her former career working in fashion. She loved clothes and had a knack for putting amazing outfits together. These days, her wardrobe consisted of leggings and long sweaters because her pants didn't fit anymore. She had dropped at least four sizes and was too thin for any of her nice clothes.

The room had been previously used as my gym, so it had a flat-screen TV mounted to the wall. She would be able to watch TV from bed if she wanted to. When we were done, it was a cozy, leafy room full of oxygen.

Kylie called both me and my mom a few times a day and was having trouble adjusting to the news. She even floated the idea of quitting her job and coming home to spend time with Grandma and help with her care. I knew she felt helpless all the way out in Colorado, but I didn't realize she was serious until I received a call early one morning.

"Mom, I bought a one-way plane ticket. I'll be there in two weeks."

"What are you talking about Kylie? This seems like a rash decision!"

"I told you about this idea, and I've been working on it for a while. I found someone to sublease my apartment, and I've arranged to put all my things in storage."

"I think we may want to talk this through a bit more. You're making a major change."

"It's too late, Mom. I've just given my two-week notice, and I'm doing this!"

"Wow, OK, sounds like you've made up your mind. I'm not sure I agree, but I will definitely appreciate the help and your grandmother will love to have you here."

My mom had been getting into a routine that we were still trying to figure out. She had been sleeping more, mostly because of the anti-anxiety drugs and sleeping pills she was taking to get through the night. I was experimenting with foods she could eat, which were soft and in small portions. I had also come up with a half-dozen variations of shakes that she could drink in the morning. They were what I called the "calorie bombs." The main ingredients were three scoops of ice cream—she preferred either vanilla or chocolate—an envelope of instant breakfast, whole milk or Ensure, and either peanut butter, chocolate syrup, strawberry syrup, Nutella, some bananas, or other fruits. It was delicious, and it was the way I got her a good number of calories in the morning along with some protein and vitamins. It might take her more than an hour to drink it all, and it always required some nagging, but she liked it and was getting it down. If she moved from the table, it was all over, so I stayed with her in the kitchen while she nursed the drink. I wish I could've joined her in sampling these delectable concoctions to show solidarity but knew my ass would soon block the sun if I got into that habit.

We weren't doing much outside the home: she was getting weaker and didn't want to see many people. It seemed that once we had this definitive diagnosis, she started a faster decline. Kent and Lorri had been over, and she talked to them on the phone as well when she felt up to it and her voice was strong. I know they were both having a ridiculously hard time with the news, and I talked to them when they needed an ear. We tried one day to get together at a restaurant in the mall, and some of the old walking group was going to join, but it failed miserably. On the way there, I looked over and she was crying silently.

"Oh no, Mom, what's the matter? Are you in pain? What's going on?"

After a minute of shuddering with her hand over her face, she finally responded, "What in the hell am I doing? I think I can just show up at a restaurant and have lunch like everything is OK? I can barely talk, let alone swallow. This is not a good idea, Julie."

"They're really looking forward to seeing you, and everyone misses you terribly, Mom."

"I can't do it. Let's just go home, please. I'm tired and just can't do this today."

"OK, no problem. Whatever you want." I handed her a tissue from the console and looked for a place to turn around. My call to Kent and Lorri was brief: I just told them that today was not a good day. They both understood and responded as if they understood it would probably never happen.

Mom needed help with some things but was still very independent. I helped her get organized before her showers, so she wouldn't fall, but she insisted on keeping her privacy in the bathroom. I put a plastic chair in our large walk-in shower so she could steady herself. The towels were placed on hooks directly by the shower door so she could easily reach them when she was through. I got a twinge of anxiety every time I left her there alone, worried that she might fall. There was often a call for me to come and help her after she was dried off and ready to get out. She was always exhausted at that point and needed some assistance. She just wasn't ready to be totally dependent, and I understood. The other main thing was getting her ready for bed. She took a lorazepam to help with anxiety and sleeping. It made her drowsy very quickly, so I made sure to get her into bed within a half-hour of taking it. I stayed in the room with her, and we talked until she fell asleep every night. It made her feel relaxed, and the time together was nice. It was quiet and she was peaceful, and we had some great discussions.

"Do you think there's an afterlife? I know we're supposed to believe in that from our religion, but what do you think, Jule?"

"I really think there is, Mom, and it helps me to think that we'll all see each other again someday. I have to believe there's something else after all of this."

With her eyes closed and fluttering to sleep, she whispered, "Well, I hope that's true, because I want to see you again someday."

Chapter 22

The Quandary

I HAD SOME THINKING to do about Friendly Neighbors. Oliver had called a few times over the past couple of days. He was checking on me and my mom, but I also knew he had some questions about my decision.

"Hi Julie, it's been a hot second since we talked. Hope all is well with your mom. Give me a call when you get a chance."

I decided I needed to at least give him an update, so I called him back via FaceTime. After four rings and a potential game of phone tag developing, he finally picked up. He was just removing his virtual reality glasses and looked sweaty.

"Hi, sorry I was slow, I just got these new glasses, and I was extreme mountain biking. It was crazy. What are you up to?"

"That sounds fun. I was just wondering how you're doing and wanted to fill you in on some recent developments."

"Cool. I've been thinking about you and your mom. How is Suzanne?" He was now noisily rummaging around in his desk drawers as he put away his virtual reality toy.

"We're doing OK, but it's been quite an adjustment. We're all just trying to adapt."

"Yeah. I can only imagine the stress that you're all dealing with." He sat down on the sofa and held up a furry little kitten in much the same way Mufasa held up Simba in *The Lion King*. "Here's something that should cheer you up. I found this little guy under the porch last night. Can you believe someone would abandon a sweet little kitten?"

"Oh no, what a little cutie. Is that something Hailey talked you into keeping?"

"No, actually, I found it before she even got here last night. What kind of asshole just kicks out a baby kitty? So, I brought him in and now we're both attached." (Long pause while he played with his furry friend.) "I named him Algorithm."

"Umm, Algorithm, huh. For a cute, fluffy kitten?"

"It was either that or Syntax, but he seems more like an Algorithm. You know, designed to solve a definite problem. I think I can use a kitten in my life."

"Well, that's great, Oliver. Congratulations on adding an actual living creature to the mix!" I laughed as I imagined him in his virtual world cuddling a purring kitten with a whack name.

"Have you been following the emails Mark's been sending to IdeaLab and the investment group?"

"Yeah, seems like he has it covered and is getting all the information. What are you thinking?" Oliver asked.

"I'm really struggling with what to do next since this might be my only chance, and I'm also procrastinating because I'm wiped out most days. My gut tells me giving up all control is a big mistake."

"Totally understandable. They could end up turning it into 'Narc On Your Neighbors' and we'd never be able to stop it. You know, an app where you take photos of all the BS your neighbors do and report it to the cops, the neighborhood association, the condo board, or anyone who might care ... just to mess with them."

He was going off on a tangent, and even though I was amused, I needed to get this back on track. "Yup, exactly. The possibilities are endless. I'm trying to think about some other finance options in between meltdowns, so I'll keep you posted. I have a couple calls into small business programs to see if there are any grants or loans for women-owned start-ups."

"Sounds good. Let me know what I can do to help."

"Maybe send up a prayer that we find some miracle. Actually, a *few* miracles would be a good strategy."

"Will do, and tell your mom I said hello, OK?"

"Thanks, Oliver. Talk soon."

Mark had handled some follow-up from the investors through calls and emails. They were starting to push hard on a final decision. I found myself thinking about it between breakfast, medications, naptime, daily entertainment planned by Ky, laundry, and other chores. I just couldn't get past working with a company whose business practices would leave me out of the pivotal decisions. But if I didn't take this offer, would I be making a big mistake? I didn't want to regret this moment, particularly since I was under duress with all that was going on in my family. I decided to use a strategy of one of my favorite childhood heroines, Scarlett O'Hara, and "think about it tomorrow because tomorrow is another day." I asked Mark to keep stalling and felt the whole opportunity slowly slipping away.

I had almost decided that the timing was just not meant to be after my inquiries for grants and loans had turned up few opportunities. Not nearly enough funds to get this project off the ground. Then one night when I was getting Suzanne comfortable in bed, she asked me how things were going with the mobile app. I didn't think she remembered the name of it, but I was surprised and proud that she recalled it was a mobile app. I told her about the offer from the investors, adding the catch about me having no say in the final product.

"That doesn't sound like what you were hoping for, Julie. Knowing you, I don't think that will work out."

"Well, you know I don't want to, but I may not have a choice."

"Why wouldn't you have a choice?" Her speech was slowing dramatically as she got more relaxed.

"Well, it takes a good amount of money to develop something like this, and right now the time and resources may not be available.

I just need to figure out another way to raise the funds, but there aren't a lot of options. And honestly, I don't care that much right now."

Her eyes were starting to flutter a little, which was the first sign the drug was taking hold. "Oh, I never told you. Kent wants to help you with this. He has been meaning to talk to you. He thinks the idea is good. I don't think I ever told you that Kent is super rich. He has all that patent money. He can help you."

She mumbled the last few words very slowly, and then she was sound asleep.

Chapter 23
The Monitor

"JULE, CAN YOU COME AND GET ME?"

I slept lightly most days and kicked off the covers abruptly as I realized she was calling me. On the advice of our visiting nurse, I got an audio baby monitor system beside my bed and her bed. The last time I had used one was when Kylie was a baby. This gave me the ability to hear her at any time without always lurking outside her door. I was usually awakened by her slurring my name at about 7:00 a.m. after we had agreed that she shouldn't get out of bed herself.

She still had the use of her arms and legs, but they were not steady. Exercises to help her gain mobility were hit or miss. One day she was a little stronger, and other days, she was as weak as a toddler. Because she might need to get into the bathroom in the early morning, I tried to get up before her, but most of the time I was so exhausted that it didn't happen. When I entered her room, she was usually sitting halfway up in bed and wide awake. I got the feeling that she laid there a while before actually calling me. I also learned that she was most depressed in the morning. She didn't speak much then and cried often.

I often tried to sidetrack her by bringing Winnie into the conversation. "Morning Wins! Did you sleep well? Did you dream about catching those horrible squirrels that taunt you every day?"

Sometimes, my mom would join in. "Were you chasing them

all night, Winnie?"

Or we talked about the weather that day. Other topics included the flowers sprouting along the woods' edge or interesting birds on the feeder, anything to distract her and keep it light.

After hitting the bathroom, the breakfast table was our first stop in the morning since I was constantly trying to get her to eat. She would try to eat scrambled eggs sometimes, but mostly, a calorie bomb shake got her going. A normal conversation usually started after she'd taken a few long pulls from her straw in the shake.

The morning after we talked about the mobile app, I wanted to follow up with her. "Hey, Mom, do you remember what we were talking about last night when you fell asleep? You really threw me for a loop!"

She paused for a second. "Oh, about that cell phone thing you are working on. Yes, I told you to talk to Kent. He's been wanting to have a discussion, but he's always so consumed with my issues that he hasn't gotten around to you yet. Is that what you mean?"

"Well, yeah, but you also said he may want to back the project financially. Do you remember that part?"

"Uh-huh." She was sipping on the shake full force now. "He has too much money and is always looking at business investments. He got paid millions for that auto patent years ago."

"Oh, holy hell, I knew he had something going on there, but he never talked about it. I can't believe he made a fortune!" I gasped.

"Yup, I found a wonderful man who wants nothing more than to travel around the world with me, and now I'm going to die. Isn't that just perfect?" She was coughing and laughing simultaneously. "He had already started making plans for us." Her voice faded as she stared out the window.

"Dammit, Mom, I'm so sorry." I hugged her from behind. "You can still travel with him. Maybe we can plan a trip right now."

"He started looking at some options, but I know I can't go.

What if I get much worse on the trip? I don't want him to deal with that mess. I have no idea what's coming down the road. It would break my heart to put him through that."

"Well, let me talk to Dr. Merrill and Kent, and we'll see if we can make something happen."

"You'd better do it soon." She leaned over and patted Winnie on the head. I couldn't tell if she was being funny or realistic, but either way, I didn't like hearing it.

Later that day Kylie showed up in the kitchen completely unannounced. I knew she was coming, but I thought she would be there on the weekend and with at least a call or a text ahead of time. She made a beeline right to her grandmother. I might as well not have even been in the room as she slid past me.

"Oh my God, Grandma, it's so good to see you! Being away from you has been torture! I'm so glad that I'm here now."

"Umm, hi, Kylie. It's me, your mother. I'm just standing here like an idiot!" They both just ignored me.

"Kylie, you're insane. You didn't have to come home. We're doing OK. I never wanted you to leave Denver ... OK, that's a lie. I'm so happy to see you, too. Oh my gosh, you look gorgeous," she slurred with tears on her cheeks.

"So do you, Grandma. I truly expected worse. You're holding it together. This is one hell of a way to get me back to Michigan." They laughed and hugged, and for a minute, the mood was bright and hopeful.

We spent the rest of the day talking about her boyfriend, Ryan, and Kent's crazy fortune, and anything but stupid ALS. It was wonderful. A few days earlier, Mom had started taking afternoon naps from 1:00–3:00 p.m. She just couldn't make it through a full day anymore. The exhaustion was evident no matter how hard she tried to hide it. After I got her settled and fully asleep, Kylie and I went back down the hall and into the kitchen. She sat on one of the island stools and looked at me, shaking her head.

"Mom, she doesn't look good at all. I am so scared." The tears started coming, and I grabbed her by the forearms.

"Look, I know this is hard. You just got here, and a lot has happened. She isn't good, and the fight is far from over. She has good days, and we're getting by. It will be great to have you here if you think you can do it. She is so happy you're here, Kylie."

"Of course, I can help. I want to be here, it's just the initial shock, I guess," Kylie said quietly.

"I know. I see her all day every day, so I'm not as aware. I know she's getting worse and I'm scared, too, but she needs us to be strong for her. We're scared, and she is more terrified than she's letting on."

"Well, this should be one hell of a shit-show team on this one, Mom." We laughed through the tears.

"Yup, the crazy bitches trying to outsmart a crazy bitch-ass disease. Oh my God, Kylie, one for the books. If I am being honest, my biggest fear is that I'm not qualified to take care of her, but there's really no guidebook for this. The visiting nurse is here two days a week to take her vitals, but she is in and out in an hour. And, she has never had an ALS patient before. So far, it's been like the blind leading the blind. I look things up on the internet and call Dr. Merrill's office and talk to the nurses, but that's the only support system I have. We went to one of the ALS clinics at Merrill's office, but she hated it and doesn't want to go back. She said it made her feel more isolated and without hope. Hospice will be available at some point, but that's the last stop, and I want to avoid that step as long as we can."

Kylie hugged me and said, "Mom, you got this. Grandma doesn't care if you don't know what you're doing. The main thing is loving her and keeping her comfortable and as happy as we can."

"You are so right, Boo. I think we need to try to get her involved in activities that she really enjoys and keep her as busy as possible, considering her energy level. Kent wants to take her on a trip, so I'm going to work on that possibility ASAP. Also, let's you and I start making a list of all her favorite things, so we can start planning daytime activities."

"That's why I'm here, Mom. Consider me in charge of the fun committee."

Kylie was in full planner mode and did a great job of setting up daily events. On Mondays, we went to the flower store and sometimes to the museum gardens, whichever Mom picked. Tuesdays were for visitors, and Kent or Lorri always stopped over and we fixed them lunch while they chatted with her in the family room. We took Mom to the matinee movies on Wednesdays. We let her pick the show, and we had to sit in the wheelchair row in the front, but nobody was ever there, so we talked and laughed at the movie as loudly as we wanted. By Thursday, she usually wanted to stay home and watch reality TV or movies on the old film channel. We also read some books together; one of her favorites was *Eat Pray Love*. I think she liked to imagine the possibilities of international travel that she knew were unlikely. The magazine choices were *People*, or worse, *The Enquirer*, which was great escapism and good for laughs. Although there was a lot of great material for expanding minds, at this point, we were keeping it breezy. On Fridays, we always tried to cook something that was an optimistic venture, like homemade pasta or pastries. The whole thing was always a disaster and never looked like the picture, but we laughed through it all, which was the point. Then we would serve the mess to Mark or visitors over the weekend and giggle at their reactions.

Taking a trip with Kent was put on hold because Mom felt the idea was too risky. Her version of *Eat Pray Love* would have to be shelved for now. She knew her health was deteriorating. Even so, there were days when we didn't talk about the disease or any of the new health issues. The one thing that amazed me was the way she always kept her perspective and sense of humor.

One evening, Kylie had left for her father's, where she was staying most nights, and Mom was snuggled in bed. After dinner, Mark had started sending me a series of sexts. They ranged from "Why are you so hot?" to "You need to get naked and in bed NOW"— not subtle.

I sauntered into the master bedroom knowing he was in there already setting the scene. The fireplace was roaring and there were a few white candles lit on the bedside tables. A great bottle of cabernet sauvignon was uncorked, and two Riedel wine glasses were keeping it company. I started to get excited. It had been a while since we had enjoyed any time alone, and it looked like it was heading in a good direction!

Mark came out of the doorway from the master bath with a cute smile on his face. "Hey, baby, so glad you could join me here."

"I got the message loud and clear, mister," I giggled.

He came over and started kissing me passionately right from the start. With everything going on, I hadn't realized how much I'd neglected him. Apparently, it had been a lot! He moved me over to the bed and had already started to pull my shirt over my head while I grabbed his and gave it a yank. I kicked off my shoes and was lying on the side of the bed as he started unzipping my jeans, kissing my neck and working down my chest. I glanced over at the wine and figured it might be "breathing" for a while.

"Julie? Julie, can you come here?" Mom's raspy voice broke through the monitor set on the side table. "I need you," she said again slowly.

We froze. "Oh, man. I better go. She needs something." I grabbed my shirt and hurriedly yanked it over my head as it caught on my earring. I zipped up my jeans while trying to smooth my hair back down.

"Oh God, Julie. Is she serious?"

"Let me just go see what she needs. I'll be right back, hold that thought." I pointed to the bed.

He laid back and I headed out the door to her room. I quickly walked in and she was still in a prone position with the covers pulled up to her chin.

"Hi, Mom, are you OK? Do you need something?"

"Yeah, I need you to stop getting some. If I can't have any, no one should, you little slut," she said, giggling.

It didn't sink in right away, but once I realized what she said, I giggled, too. "You perverted old lady, were you listening?" I gave her a light slap on the arm.

"I can't really help it. Has anyone ever told you that you're kind of loud? Maybe that's the way Mark likes it, who knows." She was slurring from the effects of her sleeping pill, but I got the meaning.

"OK, Mom, you've had your fun. I should have given you some extra drugs tonight. Do you really need something, or are you just torturing me?" I laughed.

"I couldn't resist, but I'm very sleepy. I can't imagine what I'll dream tonight!" she said.

I slapped her again and shut the door.

Chapter 24
The Picnic

SOME DAYS WERE MORE spring-like than others, and the dogwood and dandelions burst into full bloom on the edge of our woods. The trees were teeming with leaves in various states of unfurling. Little pink flowers were also popping on the flowering crabapple tree. My favorite, the redbud, set on the very edge of the yard, had pink-purple flowers that seemed to have appeared just this morning. It was going to be sixty-five degrees and the sun was back in the sky. Spring was here, and a picnic seemed in order.

Since our own backyard was so beautiful and the temperature was unseasonably high, we decided to have our first chick picnic in the yard. The idea was to get Mom outside but not go too far away. She could still walk a bit but was using the wheelchair full-time now. Her steps were unsteady, and she had fallen a few times. Each of those falls felt like an assessment of my caretaking abilities, and I took them personally. We had had a fight a few days earlier because she tried to let herself out of the bathroom and ended up on the floor. Her head barely missed the corner of the cabinet when she went down. I was scared that she was injured, but when I realized she wasn't, my immediate reaction was anger.

"Mom, what the fuck are you trying to do, get a concussion? I want you to wait for me so I can keep you from falling and getting hurt. What the hell?"

She looked at me from the floor and didn't say a word. I picked her up and while I was holding her close, we both started to cry.

"Oh shit, Mom, I'm so sorry. I should not be yelling at you. What's wrong with me?"

"No, Julie, I should listen to you. It's just—" She stopped mid-sentence. I realized she had to get it out, but I already knew what she was going to say. "It's just, I can't believe I can't do these things anymore. I can't believe I'm in this situation. I can't believe that I'm such a burden. I never wanted to be like this!"

We embraced for a long time, and she held me very tightly. After a few minutes, I said, "There is no way in hell that you are a burden. I love you so much and just want to be there for you. I am a total bitch for losing my temper. It comes from a good place. I don't want you to get hurt. It makes me look bad."

Suzanne let go and looked me squarely in the eyes. "It really is all about you, isn't it?" We both laughed, which broke the somber moment.

Kylie arrived and was determined to make the most of such a beautiful day. She arranged for the picnic in the backyard. Using a wheelchair, we were all able to get situated in a spot Ky had set up complete with large and small pillows, a blanket, and a bed tray that provided a comfy place for Mom to sit up with support. Kylie had brought out some snacks and drinks and a sippy cup for her grandma, as that was the only way she could drink anymore. We had wine, grapes, cheeses, crackers, and a variety of soft foods nicely displayed on a plate. The full spread wasn't a part of Mom's prescribed diet, but what the hell. The main goal of the picnic was normalcy. Providing a scenario that seemed as normal and natural as possible helped her to have better days. It cut down on her time on the breathing machine and the need for anxiety drugs. The day was so beautiful, it was going to take us all to a good place.

We opened the sparkling white wine and I filled two glasses and put a small amount in her cup. "Let's toast to our first official backyard picnic of the year," I said as I raised my glass and clinked with Kylie's glass and Mom's plastic cup.

"This is a real show-stopper of a spring day," Mom slurred, with way too many Ss, but we were experts at deciphering what she was saying these days.

Winnie was running back and forth in the yard like a crazed doodle. She was happy to be outside as well and was taking in all the new-season smells. It looked like she had a mother squirrel and her two small babies frozen high on a tree in the woods. She was running around the tree extremely fast and barking like crazy. We were doing our best to ignore her, but it was funny. Every so often, she would stop over and check in on my mom. She would sit awfully close to her for a few minutes, and then run off again to harass the woodland creatures.

"You know what we should do? Let's play 'You Must Dish.' Remember my rules: We pick one topic, and everyone has to chime in with some sort of contribution, no matter what the topic is." Kylie had launched this game before, and we learned many things about each other from past experiences. It's never a boring topic, and my mom usually gets annoyed with us at some point.

"Alright ladies, I get to pick the topic since it's my game. Blow jobs: yes or no?" Kylie threw it out, giggled, and then just eyed us up.

Mom did a small spit take from her sippy cup and slurred, "Wow, I guess we're going right to it today! Can't we start with, like, favorite desserts or something?"

We all laughed, and I said, "Well, I know not everyone will agree with me, but I say yes."

"Oh God, Julie, you're a complete idiot. That's what they want you to say," Mom blurted out before I had even finished.

"Who wants us to say that, Grams?" Kylie was stirring the pot.

"Who? The asshole men, that's who." The way she slurred her Ss was hilarious and we all slumped over on the blanket, cracking up. She even giggled, which was great.

"OK, so it's some kind of male conspiracy? The whole blow job concept?" I directed this to Mom.

"Well yes, they came up with the whole idea and they really like it when we're on our knees. That's their preferred position. We are beneath them, subservient." (Again, with the slurred Ss.) "It's a complete power play." She was on a roll. "They just make us believe that it's part of regular sex when they know it is all about power. I blame the ignorant French ladies. They fell for the idea that started this whole mess."

"I don't know, Grams. I'm not sure men are really that smart and, also, it seems like we get reciprocal acts from them, too, so how is it all about power?" Kylie wondered.

"Oh Kylie, that's all part of the plan. Men don't mind doing disgusting things. They're basically animals anyway. They've been working on this for centuries. Hell, it's a win-win for them. They don't have to do any of the work, *and* they get all the reward!"

We were all laughing now, sipping our wine, and having fun. Mom was even drinking some from her cup. The day was great, and we moved on from that intellectual conversation to all sorts of other topics. The stimulating chatter kept us all from thinking about naps and drugs and other depressing things.

"Hey, Grandma, I thought about something the other day when I was at the gym. Remember when my mom signed us all up for that workout place that was a circuit where you went around and did different machines? Then they rang a bell, and everyone switched?"

"Yes, I remember that. Your mom thought we were getting to be lazy fat asses and signed us up without our consent."

"Umm, I'm right here and can hear you guys. I thought it would be some good bonding time to work out together, so sue me." I was always getting flak from these two when I tried to get them involved in healthy things.

"Grams, do you remember the time you almost got in a fight with that lady on the treadmill?" Kylie was giggling.

"Oh yes, the one who was getting a cupcake recipe from her friend on the phone? She was hogging the machine and not paying any attention to the bell because she was so interested in that damn cupcake recipe. It was like stuffed cupcakes or something ridiculous." She couldn't pronounce ridiculous, but we knew what she meant.

"Oh my God, Grams, you walked right up to her and told her it was time to move but she didn't pay any attention. She kept repeating, 'Oh, so it's cream cheese and butter mixed with the sugar.' We were all laughing, and she didn't even notice. She just kept repeating the decadent ingredients while she walked super slow on the treadmill."

"That woman was not committed to slimming down. I was doing her a favor," Mom slowly added. She was starting to get tired, and her eyes were drooping. We had been out at the picnic for a couple hours now, and she needed some rest.

"That was a classic. I don't think we ever saw her back at the gym after that day. Cupcakes won. Mom, are you getting a little tired? Do you want to go in and lie down?" I asked gently.

"Oh no, this is too fun. I want to stay out here."

So, we stayed out for another half hour and watched Winnie bark at the squirrels, the flowers sprout, and the world seemed right this day. If only we could freeze time. Mom dozed off a few times and seemed happy just being outside with us. Ky and I looked at each other and silently noted that watching her sleep so peacefully was as if nothing had ever happened. We sat like that in a beautiful, gauzy haze until I noticed Mark out of the corner of my eye coming up from the yard near the driveway.

"Hey ladies, this looks dangerous. I see there has been some wine consumed here," he said.

"Oh yeah, we've had a great afternoon," Mom responded, popping up like a Jack-in-the-box.

"It's such a beautiful day to be outside, and I'm afraid I have to spoil it and get Julie on a conference call about Friendly Neighbors," he said, turning to me.

"Oh, I didn't know we were having a call. Who is it with?"

"I just talked to Oliver, and we need to get a few things organized, so it will be the three of us if you have the time," Mark said.

"Yes, we were going to head in soon anyway. I'm sure Kylie can handle moving the picnic indoors."

"No prob, Mom. Grams and I will handle it."

I went inside with Mark and we headed to the upstairs office. Mark started filling me in as we climbed the stairs. "Oliver has been great at helping to handle all the loose ends and move this along. I told him we're not going to go with the current investment group, and he agreed. He mentioned that they seem like they want to skip a few key steps to get this to market fast. He doesn't think they're clear on all the testing that needs to take place to make it a quality product, and of course, we are out on any say in the final piece."

"OK, I'm glad he thought it through. So, if not them, then what's the plan?" I asked.

"Let's get him on the phone and talk about the options." Mark seemed to be on a mission.

We called Oliver and chatted for a few minutes about everything that had been going on with the app. I felt a little guilty; I had been staying out of it on purpose because my mother's care was taking all my time and I was too overloaded to think about much else.

"Well, I have some news, and I wanted to tell you both at the same time," Mark announced. "I have had a few meetings with Kent and both teams of attorneys, and he has agreed to be the sole financial backer of Friendly Neighbors. He'll be putting up all the money to get us into a prototype and testing. He also agreed to a sizable operations and marketing budget with us in the driver's seat. And the best part is, he only wants a 50 percent share, an equal split. There's no way that we could have found a better program or a more hands-off partner. It's a great deal."

"What the hell? When did all of this happen?" I was in shock.

"I chatted with Suzanne after she mentioned it to you and then talked to him many times over the past few weeks, and he is fully committed. I hope you don't mind, Julie, but I wanted to handle this for you and make it a surprise."

"A surprise? Wow, Mark, mission accomplished! I thought we were starting over with funding." Oliver apparently was out of the loop as well since there was silence on his end.

This meant that the product would still be in our control, and we had the right amount of financing to make it happen. It was going to get done, and I couldn't believe it! All our work and plans were going to actually *be* something. Oliver was a big part of this, and I knew there was something else that needed to be accomplished.

"Oliver, we need to do some talking. I'm going to need you to take over the project for a while. Do you think you could do that? Of course, we'll make you an officer of the company with all the rights and benefits that come with that. We will get to work on a contract. What do you think?" I asked.

There was silence and then, "Ummm, YES! That is amazing, Julie! I'd be stoked to take that role. But only until you're ready to get fully involved again."

"That may be a little while, and you'll be handling a great deal for me. Thanks so much, Oliver."

I had tears in my eyes thinking that there were so many wonderful people in this world willing to make dreams come true. I was so excited to have my creation back on track and moving forward; however, a twinge of guilt remained in the battle between success and wanting to give all I could to caring for my mom.

Chapter 25
The Dinner

THERE'S A FAVORITE PHOTO of my mom, her four sisters, and her mother sitting on a sofa with their legs crossed in the same direction. I would guess the year to be around 1965, during some special occasion or holiday, and they all look gorgeous. They have beautifully coiffed hair, are wearing stylish dresses, and they look happy. In most family group shots, you get a sense of inner personal struggles if they exist, but in this one, there is only pure joy. My mom loved this photo as much as I did, because it portrayed happier times.

I felt it was my responsibility to get her big family of siblings together with her again before it was too late. She wanted no part of this idea, but I think she knew that it would be the last time she would see them. She had started counting the "lasts": last Christmas, last Mother's Day, last birthday ... she kept it quiet, but I could see her mind working on these final morbid scenarios of life ending.

"I really don't want them all looking at me and worrying that I will drop at any minute." She had a flair for dramatic and complex relationships that I would surely never understand.

"That's probably the only reason they would come, to see just how bad it is."

"What the hell are you even talking about, Mom? Maybe, just maybe they really want to see you and have a nice time. I know they're concerned because I talk to them, but they're coming from love, not some sick curiosity." I shrugged, knowing she really wasn't listening to me.

She was focused on throwing a ball across the family room for Winnie to retrieve. The ball was only going three or four feet a throw, and this simple task seemed to be an effort. It was difficult watching her body struggle to perform acts that were practically effortless only a few months ago. Even playing fetch with Winnie was a chore.

"How about we whip up a simple dinner, have them all over for a few hours, and that will be it? I can't keep putting them off. They've all asked to visit. Getting them here in one group will be easier for you." I was trying to appeal to her general sense of negativity toward her siblings since getting it over quickly would most likely sound good to her.

"OK. Julie, you've worn me down. I'll do it. When were you thinking?"

"This coming Saturday will work for them. How about 3 o'clock?" I quickly said.

"You already invited them, didn't you?" At least her intuition was intact.

"Yes, you are correct. I've been working on the plan for a few weeks."

"You really are a brat, Julie. You know that, right?" She gave a hard swallow after getting the words out. It was getting harder to talk.

"Yes, I know." I smiled and gave her a side hug as she continued to focus on the ball covered with dog slobber.

Over the years, my mom has told me numerous stories about her childhood. The bad times (as she called them) started when her father died in a horrific car accident. He was riding to work with some neighbors when a truck carrying steel beams lost its load in front of them. Beams came crashing through the windshield. He was killed instantly. My grandmother was suddenly a young widow with eight small children, a large farm, and little savings. She was inconsolable and stayed in bed for weeks. My mom remembered the relatives who had come to help would gather for hushed talks about potentially splitting up the children. Eventually, my grandmother got out of bed, pulled herself together, went back to school, and became a secretary. She got a job with an insurance company and worked her way up to office manager. She single handedly put food on the table, saved the farm, and kept the children together. True grit.

During that time, the kids were mainly unsupervised and raised each other. My mom was one of the younger children, and my Aunt Lois was assigned to keep track of her—but didn't do a good job since she had concerns of her own. My mom says they ran like wild animals, often hid on the farm property, sometimes slept in the barn, and were cold and dirty. She told me that she and Kink had lice so bad once that they went to the barbershop and had all their hair cut off. The farmhouse was drafty, and in the winter, the frozen water in the toilet had to be broken before it could flush. Not happy times, and she resented her mother and her older siblings for the issues that caused her insecurities and depression. I heard her argue about this with my Aunt Karen, who was older and didn't remember it like that at all.

I talked to Aunt Karen about the visit, and she was able to coordinate a date for herself and the other four. Seven of the eight siblings were still living, following the death of Mom's Irish twin sister, Kink. My Aunt Margaret was in the hospital for a stroke. But her other siblings, Aunt Lois, Uncle James, Aunt Karen, Uncle Mitch, and Uncle Ed would be able to make it.

I made a few appetizer platters and stocked up on wine and hard liquor since that is often the key to a successful family gathering. Mostly for myself. Mark volunteered to make a great dinner. Hopefully, the day would go off without a hitch. What could possibly go wrong?

Mom was not having a good day, and I could tell she didn't

want visitors. But it was too late. They all had at least a two-hour drive to get to my house and were already on their way. I suggested she take a nap so that she might feel more up to the visit when they arrived at 3:00. She told me to "fuck off." Kylie giggled. She loved to hear my mom treat me like a child. But then Ky talked to her, and they went into my room to lie on the king-sized bed.

Mark prepared lamb chops with rosemary and a few side dishes, and I put together a salad and a cheesecake. We were both drinking red wine in the kitchen and bracing ourselves for the "festivities." It seemed my mom had a way of stirring up trouble with her siblings. The last time she had been with all of them was a few Christmases earlier when she stood up and declared that she would not host the holiday on her upcoming turn and that she was "canceling Christmas." She had used the fake Costco job to avoid all group get-togethers since then.

The first to arrive were my Aunt Karen and Aunt Lois. It was around 2:45 and Mom had not gotten up yet, so I sent Kylie to go and get her, gently.

"Oh my gosh, Julie, I love that table! It's Baker, isn't it?" She was looking right past me into the dining room. My Aunt Lois and her husband had owned a high-end furniture store for over forty years, so this comment was certainly on brand.

"Yes, Aunt Lois, it is, and Mark brought it to the marriage. I would never buy something that nice, but he's a bit fancy, as you know." I shrugged my shoulders; she wasn't really listening since she was busy shoving her coat at me while heading to the table for further inspection.

"Hi, Aunt Karen," I said, turning to give her a hug.

"Hi, sweet Jule, I'm so happy to see you. How have you been doing?" Aunt Karen was giving me a concerned look like she was assessing the stress on my face. She was my godmother and the next closest mother figure in the family to me. Once a week, she called me just to check. She always took the extra time to let me know how much the family appreciated the care that I was giving to my mom.

"You know, I'm doing OK, just making sure she's doing OK. Or as well as she can."

Right on cue, Kylie and Mom came around the corner. Mom was using the walker instead of the wheelchair, which I took as a sign that she was feeling stronger today. Winnie was right behind them and ran to Aunt Karen and attempted to rip her sweater. Even in that commotion, the foyer became eerily quiet as her sisters took a long look. As they grew quiet and stared at Mom, I realized that this was the first time they'd seen her drastic change in appearance. The last time they saw her, she weighed about 180 pounds. Now she was scarcely 100. She also had thinning hair that we curled to make it look fuller. Her skin tone was gray and covering it with makeup just gave it an odd, washed-out peachy color. Her eyes had a vacant look and her eyelids drooped.

Not only had her appearance changed, but so had her mobility. The muscles in her legs and neck were not getting all the signals from the brain anymore and she walked/shuffled at a slow pace. Her neck was too weak to hold up her head, so when she got the least bit tired, her chin went down to her chest. She often wore a neck pillow during the day, like the ones sold in airports. She was self-conscious about it, so she didn't have it on for the dinner. I knew her head would be down to her chest before this visit concluded. She held steady eye contact with her sisters as she shuffled in. I know her so well. She was enjoying the shock factor.

Aunt Karen gently pushed Winnie aside and rushed over to Mom. "Hi, Suz, it's wonderful to see you."

Mom grabbed her around the neck for a hug, but it almost looked for a minute like she might fall forward trying to lift her arms. She didn't, but it was very awkward and my Aunt Karen, all 120 pounds herself, struggled a little to get her balance and place Mom's hands back on the walker grips.

"I'm so glad you're here, Karen." Mom had a tear in her eye, and I knew she missed her sisters much more than she admitted.

"Oh my gosh, Suzy, you are so thin!" my Aunt Lois said with

her usual lack of decorum. I can't imagine the things she must say to the shoppers at her store.

"Hi, Lois, thanks for noticing. I've been on this new diet. It's called slow death," Mom said.

Kylie and I couldn't control the laugh that escaped and then caught ourselves. Mom got a kick out of zinging Lois. She always told me that many of her issues came from the horrible care—neglect, even—from her childhood. Lois denied it, but who knows the truth? It was a terrible situation, kids taking care of kids, no matter who was to blame.

"OK, that's enough of that. Let's go sit in the living room and have some appetizers. What can I get you two? I have soft drinks, some nice red or white wine, or a cocktail?" I was determined to refocus them by moving to a new location ... and alcohol could only help.

"Wine sounds good to me, Julie. Either kind." Aunt Karen was helping Mom into a chair in the living room, visibly shaken from the comment and her appearance.

"Sure, Julie. I'll have some red," Aunt Lois said as she recovered from the harsh death comment that had at least broken the ice.

"Why don't you guys chat a bit, and I'll be right back with some appetizers. Kylie, do you want to help me carry some things?"

"Sure, I'll be back, ladies. Please behave for five minutes." Kylie directed it right at my mom, who grinned.

I was glad to see Mom might enjoy the day, even if it meant we had to put up with whatever the sick lady might say. She knew she had a license to offend, and there was nothing anybody would do about it.

The doorbell rang as I headed to the kitchen. I doubled back to find my mom's three brothers standing together on the front porch like a trio of former vacuum cleaner salesmen. James was the oldest at eighty, Mitch was seventy-two, and Ed was sixty-nine.

"Hi, Julie, sorry we're late. We decided to ride together, and I took a wrong turn at the stop sign down there. It's somewhat confusing because you have two driveways," Uncle Ed explained.

"He insisted on using the Navigation Nanny, and it sent us in the wrong way. I prefer to use good old-fashioned folding maps. You can trust those," Uncle James added.

"No worries. I know, it's hard to find since we have two driveways, and the front one is very steep. It's a corner lot, so we live off both streets. Glad you made it OK and you're not late at all. The sisters are just getting organized in the living room." I kissed them all and took their coats.

I motioned them toward the living room and decided to let them greet Mom on their own. I was already stressed from anticipating what she might say. It was best to just go about my business and help Mark get dinner together.

Kylie was in the kitchen rehashing the "slow death diet" comment with Mark.

"It's probably really fun for her to have the upper hand with Lois. I mean, what is Lois going to do, fight with the ill sister?" Mark laughed as he stirred the sauce.

"Grandma has that look on her face where she knows she's going to stir up some shit today," Kylie said.

"Hopefully not too much, and with any luck, she'll soon be too tired to make much trouble," I said.

You could set a watch by her schedule these days. Up at 10:00 a.m., nap at 1:00 p.m., up at 3:00 p.m., dinner at 5:00 p.m., bed by 8:00 p.m. When she was awake, she was weak and wanted to sit and talk a little, pet Winnie, or watch her favorite TV shows. Her speech was not good, and when she was tired, it became extremely slurred. I knew she had about one good hour with her siblings before she would become exhausted.

I found out that the brothers wanted beers and we took all the drinks and two large appetizer platters into the living room. They were making small talk about the usual stuff: the weather, spouses, kids, anything but my mom's situation. I decided to sit and be social for a minute.

"Julie, I love your house. I've never been here before since we missed the housewarming party you had when you moved in. The setting is really peaceful," Uncle Mitch said.

"We love being in the woods and not seeing our neighbors. The lots are all a couple acres, so we're spread out. It's been a really nice house for us."

"Suzy, you must love living here, too." Mitch turned to her.

"Yes, it's beautiful. I just wish that I could enjoy it more instead of worrying if I'm going to wake up in the morning." She paused for effect and watched her siblings' reactions. I noticed a slight look of horror on most of their faces. This would be her entertainment for today, it seemed.

"Mom, you're such a crazy joker. You really should lay off the dark humor. They just got here. Maybe give it a rest," I whispered to her and emphasized the last part with a hard stare.

"I'm just being funny guys. Sorry." She slurred the words since she was already running out of energy. They smiled and moved on to talk about things like Ed's latest grandchild.

I realized we needed to get dinner on the table fast. I went into the kitchen and gave Mark and Kylie an update on the conversation.

"We need to pick up the pace so we can wrap this up. She's in rare form."

"Got it. We can eat in ten minutes." Mark moved into action.

"I'll set the table. Mom, do you want them all in the dining room?" Kylie asked while grabbing some plates from the buffet cabinet.

"Let's put them at the kitchen table; it's a little more casual. That might lighten the mood." I went back into the living room to give them a timeline update. "Hi guys, it looks like dinner will be ready in ten minutes."

"Oh, very nice, Julie. I can't wait to see what Mark will be surprising us with today." Aunt Karen had been a guest for many Sunday dinners and always commented that the food was exceptional. We haven't had them since my mom moved in.

"Hey, Julie, give us an update on that computer mobile gadget you are working on. I heard about it from Steve, and it sounded interesting. Is it for older people, like my brothers?"

"Oh, wow, I forgot I talked to Cousin Steve about it. It's called Friendly Neighbors, and it's focused on connecting people who need household help with people who are available in their neighborhood to provide the help. Yes, it's moving along. It looks like we just got some financing to build and test the prototype. We just took on an equal partner to help keep it going. It's exciting to watch it develop. And, yes, it's perfect for all of you!"

"That sounds great. We're wishing you all the luck in the world. I don't really understand it, but it sounds great." Aunt Karen was always so sweet and encouraging.

"Thanks, guys. Now if you don't mind, let's move to the kitchen." I went over and helped Mom out of the chair and into the wheelchair I had waiting nearby in the corner.

As I pulled her up, she whispered, "I am glad to see them, Julie, even if it doesn't seem like it."

"Oh, Mom," I said with an exaggerated smile, "let's go get some dinner." She knew I couldn't react since everyone was right there.

Mark, Kylie, and I ate in the dining room so the siblings could talk. When I went into the kitchen to refill wine and water glasses and see if they needed anything, they were discussing the farm where they grew up and some of their childhood neighbors.

"Do you remember that Halloween party the Boldens used to have? They lived right next to the town cemetery, and it was so scary to go over there," Aunt Karen said.

"I loved it! We would hide in the bushes and scare the girls as they left," Uncle Ed commented.

"I heard that Lonny Bolden is in the hospital and not doing very well. Of course, he's got to be well into his 80s by now. He was kind of a pervert as I recall," Aunt Lois said, muttering the last part under her breath.

Mom was quiet. She was getting tired and had lost some of her fight. I saw the concern on Aunt Karen's face and gave her a weak smile as I headed over.

"Mom, did you try to eat anything?" I had chopped up ridiculously small pieces of meat, hoping they would be easier to swallow. I had also piled her plate with mashed potatoes and applesauce, so she could attempt to eat with her family.

"No, Julie, I'm too sleepy," she mumbled.

"OK, Mom, maybe we could move you to the sofa to rest?"

She slowly shook her lowered head, and I knew she had had enough. "I'm going to help her into the bedroom for a nap. Does that sound good, Mom?"

She nodded yes and held out her hand. I looked around the table, and it was noticeably quiet. They jumped up one by one to give her a hug and say goodbye.

Chapter 26
The Days

I WOKE UP THAT MORNING thinking about a ball field we had in our backyard as kids. The path to all the bases was worn and the grass was gone. We had used it so much that it became a permanent ball diamond where we played softball, kickball, and wiffleball all summer long. It was the place that the whole neighborhood gathered, and it was usually a rowdy spot. I know being the neighborhood hangout wore on my mom's nerves because every so often she declared a "no ball today" moratorium, but that was a rare occurrence. I think she liked knowing where her kids were and having us in our own yard was the best. I appreciate things like this now, and realize she did a lot for us. I was brought back from that pleasant memory by her weak voice on the monitor.

"Jule, can you come?"

Each day started the same, but what came as the day went on was unpredictable. The disease was making its presence known a little more with each sunrise, and that brought new challenges. I researched a lot and belonged to a few online groups that were specifically for caregivers, but that wasn't enough. Our visiting nurse had never had an ALS patient before, so she did the best she could but often didn't have an answer. So, after some calls and an assessment, hospice finally assigned us a nurse named Molly. She specialized in ALS and began coming to the house three days a week to do my mom's vitals and talk to us about challenges and what advice and resources she could offer. She didn't stay long, and I knew that was because Mom had a lot of support in our house. I was always there, and Kylie was there quite a few days a week. Mark was around when he could work from home, and he always pitched in at night. Molly had other patients who didn't have the resources and comfort of family around to care for them. She was needed more urgently elsewhere.

Molly was due for a visit one morning, and I wanted to discuss breathing issues. Mom was getting increasingly short of breath. It scared her so much that sometimes she would hyperventilate. That started a downward spiral that ended with me soothing her, having her breathe into a paper sack, and then moving her to the BiPAP machine. That required her to wear a mask, which would often trigger her claustrophobia and panic attack all over again.

Molly suggested a drug called Ativan, in liquid form, to calm her down when this happened. Ativan was used to treat anxiety disorders, trouble sleeping, and many other serious issues for ALS patients. She promised to bring it the next day after she talked to the hospice doctor. She also mentioned another drug, Riluzole, that could help ALS patients by slowing the progression and possibly extending their life by a few months.

Mom just looked blankly at Molly and said with a slur, "I don't want anything that may add a few months. I know what the result will be. A few more months of hell isn't what I'm hoping for. I know you need to tell me about it, but no thanks."

Molly understood, gave her a quick hug, and confirmed the next visit in a few days.

Since the morning had been so draining, it was time for Mom to get some rest. Even though it was a little earlier than the usual nap time, she was exhausted.

"Mom, do you want to go to the bathroom before we get you into bed?"

"Yeeh." Her speech was clipped since she saved her words when she was tired. The slurring was getting worse, so she kept the word count down when she could. Also, I knew it frustrated her to be asked this kind of question about using the bathroom. She was losing more privacy each day.

The bathroom process had changed a little because I was always worried about her falling. She wanted to be alone, which was understandable, so I put her on the toilet and shut the door, leaving it open a crack. Since I was the only one home, I wanted to stay close to her. She promised not to get up until she called me so I could help her from there. We were doing the best we could considering the situation. This time, she was there for a long time, so I knocked lightly.

"Hey, Mom, are you OK?" I thought maybe she had fallen asleep on the toilet, which had happened the previous day.

"Not really, Jule." I barely understood what she said because it was a whisper, and she was whimpering.

"I'm coming in." I found her still on the toilet but looking up at me with tears in her eyes.

"I have diarrhea. It won't stop. I don't know what to do."

"That's OK, Mom, no problem. I'm going to get some Imodium and some juice. I'll be right back, OK?" I had learned to manage my responses no matter what happened. I knew she was taking cues from me and that it was important to keep her calm.

I came back to the bathroom with a crushed Imodium pill, a drink, and a warm washcloth and towel for any potential cleanup. She was still on the toilet but had dozed off. "Mom, I'm going to lift you up. Is that OK?"

She nodded sleepily and looked up at me. I eased her up with one hand and steadied myself on the countertop with the other. The situation went from bad to worse, and Mom suddenly began to cry so loud that it startled me, and I almost lost my grip. I quickly moved her to lean on the sink cabinet while I grabbed towels within reach.

The whole time I said, "It's OK, we can deal with it. Please don't cry, Mom."

She must have felt horrible having to depend on her own daughter in that way. I was just prioritizing, with my focus on cleaning her up. The episode finally ran its course. I had her wrapped in the towel and suggested I give her a quick shower. She was just too tired, so we opted to get her to bed and try a sponge bath. She nodded, and I wiped her tears. We looked at each other, and she grabbed onto me tighter than she ever had. She leaned into me with all her weight, which wasn't much.

"I'm so scared. I'm losing this battle." Her speech was hard to decipher, but the message was clear. She was rapidly losing the battle against the invisible monster that ravaged her body.

"Oh, Mom, please try not to worry. I'm here, and I'm going to be here. I'll be with you."

She slept through the last part of the sponge bath. I covered her with three blankets and closed the door to her room. Then I quietly got the bathroom cleaned and disinfected and headed toward the kitchen. I slipped into the half bath off the hall, slumped down to the cold tile floor, and sobbed.

What the fuck was I thinking? This was a battle for her life, and we already knew we were going to lose. There was no treatment or possibility of remission for ALS. It just slowly marched down a path that ended with the inevitable. I may not be equipped to do this, let alone have all the responsibility for her care. How did I even think this was something that I could handle? I couldn't handle it. I was a complete weak-ass idiot! I was in over my head.

Over the next few days, Mom seemed a little better. There were fewer episodes with the BiPAP machine. She was awake, and more importantly, alert for longer periods. In fact, one day I was in the kitchen, and she came buzzing around the corner with her walker, moving very swiftly. She had balance and was enjoying cruising around the first floor. She still struggled with breathing problems at times, but they were fewer and farther between. She wasn't eating much, but she did seem better. Of course, it was up and down, and I wondered when the disease would saunter back in and take all this progress away, as it always did, but we tried to enjoy the moments.

At her request, the three of us had another picnic in the yard and talked about all the beautiful places where she had traveled.

"You know my favorite place to visit was London. I just love it there." Her eyes lit up as she thought about the trip. She was very upbeat and animated, even though she struggled to get some words out.

"Your father took me on that business trip. He was so busy, and I had a lot of time on my own." There was a long pause as she rested and had a drink of juice from the sippy cup. We sat patiently; I could tell she wanted to talk today, even if it was a huge chore. "I went to the London Zoo. I saw a huge silverback gorilla that lived with two females. He was so intelligent looking and stared right into my eyes. I really felt like we were communicating, or that he was contemplating how to kill me. I couldn't decide."

We all laughed. "I remember you talking about that, Mom, and all the other exotic animals. You mentioned that day at the zoo was one of your favorite times even though you were alone." I tried to fill in some time while she regrouped to tell us more of the story.

"Yes, but my favorite place was the butterfly house. It was newly built and had large groups of butterflies that fluttered through the house and landed on flowers."

She was whispering slowly as her voice gave out, and we struggled to hear her but let her finish the thought. After more sips of water and a few minutes of rest, she continued.

"The flower gardens in London are beautiful. I went to tea in the most amazing garden I have ever seen."

At this point, she was so tired that I wanted to help her with the conversation. "I can picture this garden because I remember you describing it, Mom. It had every color of perennial and stunning cascades of roses. You ate finger sandwiches and pastries, and I remember you saying that the scent of the flowers was heavenly."

"Yes, that garden gave me the inspiration to turn my yard into an English-style garden."

We could tell that the last point made her a little sad since she hadn't been to her own house in several weeks. I am sure the gardens needed some spring attention, but no one had the energy to check them out.

We lifted her spirits by changing the subject to talk about vacations on Sanibel Island on the Gulf side of Florida that we had taken as a family for many years. We loved the shells that rolled up onto the beach each day, and the perfect weather in the mid-80s. We talked about the island beaches and the clattering noises the sudsy surf made when it hit the endless piles of shells. That did the trick. Mom fell back into a relaxed state, and we helped her to the bedroom for a nap.

While she was resting, I used the time to call my brothers and sister. They wanted to come to see Mom and give me a break to go out of town with Mark. It was hard for them to not be there regularly with all that was happening to their mother. Also, they didn't think I was getting enough rest, and frankly, I agreed since I felt exhausted and was looking forward to a break. Jeff and YuMei were coming Friday afternoon, and Jon, Hannah, and Jenny were arriving Saturday morning. Mark and I were going to Chicago for a weekend escape. Kylie would stay at the house to help with any questions that came up, but I wasn't going to leave anything to chance and started making detailed instructions and lists.

The medication list was first, and it went through each segment of the day and detailed the drug name, color, description, and quantity. These drugs covered any and all scenarios from blood pressure to anti-anxiety to non-secretion tablets to antidepressants. Their usage was modified about every three or four days depending on how Mom was doing. The list I made for them was meant to cover any possible issues through Sunday. If they needed more info, they could always call me. The process for giving pills was also in the instructions since they needed to be crushed and stirred into a very small amount of liquid. We found through trial and error that using two large spoons was the simplest way to crush the pills. Also, some needed to be cut in half depending on the current dosage. If we gave her too much liquid in the mixture, she couldn't swallow it all and wouldn't get the full dose of the drug, so it needed to be precise.

Then came the basic schedule plan. I called it a plan because it was often a guideline instead of law. Mom still wanted to have some say in her world, so we had deviations. I detailed the routines for morning, afternoon, and nighttime. There was also a food sheet. This was detailed by time of day as well. It was extremely specific because I was always fighting the food battle. She rarely ate much anymore, so any trick I found to add just a few more calories was included. I was forever trying to get snacks between the meals, and she had some weak spots—pudding and ice cream treats—that could be used as enticements. Also, keeping a high-calorie beverage in a sippy cup with her always helped to get in a few extra calories throughout the day. All the rules I'd used to try and cut my own calories were imposed in the opposite direction. I often felt the lack of food was going to be the knockout punch in this fight. She never wanted a feeding tube, but she grew thinner every day as her appetite decreased.

There was one item I made sure to talk to all of them about, and that was the bedtime schedule. I had learned the hard way that it needed to be precise or the whole thing went awry. At around 8:00 p.m., you crush the nighttime pills and put the dust in a small amount of juice. Then take her into her bathroom to help her wash her face, brush her teeth, and get on pajamas. The teeth and face were getting less attention from her in her routine. She was just running out of energy, but it didn't seem a big concern for any of us. Next, have her drink the liquid/pill mixture. This needed to happen around 8:15 since she would be exhausted. Promptly get her into bed in the next fifteen minutes because once the pills took over, she would start to lose consciousness and it would be impossible to get her there without carrying her. Like I said, I learned that the hard way.

The weekend went well on both fronts. Mark insisted that we try to refocus since the daily routine was impacting all of us, and I agreed. He planned some nice dinners with great wine which was wonderful. We also spent a good amount of time in our beautiful hotel room, barely dressed, with champagne in bed and a stunning view of the river. It was nice to be a couple again without all the routines at home that took us in other directions. But I still found it extremely hard to relax. My family was completely capable of giving Mom good care, but somehow, I felt guilty. I kept wondering if everything was going OK back home. I found myself worrying and texting more than I should. Most of the texts occurred as I lingered in the bathroom because Mark wanted me to try to relax and recharge. They sent me some photos and selfies. Mom looked so fragile in the photos. We came home a little early on Sunday and had a nice dinner before my sister and brothers headed back to their towns a few hours away. It was so wonderful to have them spend time with Mom. She was tired from all the activity and went to bed even earlier.

That night, I woke up to very loud talking on the monitor. It was her voice, but she wasn't calling for me. I couldn't make out what she was saying, but she was obviously communicating. It was like a one-sided conversation with silences between her short sentences. I got up and went into the hall, investigating through the crack in her doorway. She was sitting up in bed and talking very clearly to a space at the end of the bed.

"Mom, are you OK? Do you need to get up and go to the bathroom?" I pushed open the door. She stopped talking but didn't turn my way. I walked over to the bed. "Hi, Mom, do you need me?"

She finally turned to me and a soft glow from the window lit up her face. "Julie, I was talking to Kink. She was here."

I froze. She looked very calm and said it as if it were a fact.

"Mom, what do you mean? You just said you were talking to Kink. Do you mean your sister?"

"Yes, it was Kink. She was here." She motioned to the bottom of the bed. "She came to talk to me about going with her."

"Oh, were you dreaming?" I was looking for any rational explanation because she was very matter of fact, and it was unsettling in that moment.

"Not dreaming; she was here. It was so great to see her. She was talking to me about going with her. I told her I wanted to go with her, but I wasn't ready yet. It was a wonderful talk. I have missed her for so long." She lay back on her pillow and closed her eyes at that point. And just like that, she was asleep.

I stood frozen to the floor.

Chapter 27
The Priest

THE STORY ABOUT MY MOM'S deceased sister confused me, and I wasn't sure what to make of it all. She didn't bring it up again and neither did I, so we left it at that, but I was glad to see that it seemed to comfort her.

Molly had mentioned at the last visit that she thought it would be a good time to get the doctor to the house to see Mom. The few weeks of improvement had come to a halt and Mom was now dealing with another bladder infection, coughing attacks, and dizziness. She had even passed out a few times while sitting in her wheelchair. The last time she fell she was in the kitchen, and she landed on the hardwood floor and hit her head. Mark was out of town and Kylie was not back from seeing her dad. It's amazing how quickly you become desensitized to horrible situations when you encounter them regularly. You adjust your "normal" and move forward.

I called 911 and had paramedics there within minutes. When I told them she had ALS, they gave us both an incredibly sad look, said how sorry they were, and did the best they could to assess the situation. She wasn't seriously injured, so we opted not to take her to the hospital for treatment. I only called them because she was unconscious for a few seconds, and I was not able to lift her. After that, I started to make sure I was always with her because she would not use the restraints to avoid falling. She just didn't care.

I overheard Molly talking to a Dr. Phillips on the phone. Doctor visits were rare unless there was a specific reason, so I was curious to find out why he had decided to come by. He had more than twenty years of experience dealing with ALS patients, so I was interested to hear his thoughts.

He went right over to my mom and greeted her. "Hello, Suzanne, I'm glad to meet you. Molly has been keeping me updated. How are you doing today?"

"Hi doctor, I'm OK today, but not great." She was sitting on the sofa in the family room with her neck pillow on, and she looked exhausted.

He assessed her with a look and kept his questions direct and to the point. "Are you able to sleep at night? Molly mentioned you're having breathing issues."

"I sleep OK, but I notice it's hard to breathe sometimes, and I panic."

"I understand. Are you anxious a lot?"

"Yes, I am. I'm scared most of the time."

I felt myself start to tear up. She looked so frail today, and I felt so helpless in my ability to comfort her fears.

"Have you been experiencing any severe cramps or pain in any of your muscles?"

"Yes, sometimes, and my daughter massages my legs, which helps." She looked over at me, and I hoped she didn't see my watery eyes.

After this session went on for half an hour, he took out a notepad and made some notes.

"I want to start you on liquid morphine. You can have it every two to three hours for coughing and pain. This will provide immediate relief and give you peace so you can rest easy. We will also treat the bladder infection. I think that Ritalin could help if you need energy. You can take it as needed."

He then looked at me to confirm the new drugs, since he knew I was her main caregiver, before turning back to my mom. "Suzanne, you don't need to be worried or scared. We're going to make sure you are calm and comfortable." He got up, went over, and patted my mom's hand.

I had the feeling that Dr. Phillips had said this exact thing maybe hundreds of times. He'd made that same hand-patting motion dozens of times. I wondered if he was aware of how comforting that was or if it was just instinctual.

After he gave me all the instructions and his numbers so I could reach him at any time, he left. Molly was still there and told us what a nice man he was and how she enjoyed working with him. She also mentioned that now he would be available to us anytime we needed to call him. This seemed like a good thing but a very scary indicator. We had moved on to a new phase.

After her nap that day, Mom had a request. She wanted to go see her priest at the church. Father Rich had been to the house before to give her communion, but this time, she wanted to go visit him. She didn't want to go to mass, but just to speak to him in his office. I didn't know exactly what prompted her request but felt I needed to make it happen. I called his secretary and found out that we could come that day if we arrived before 5:00 p.m. because he had confirmation classes that night.

Getting her ready to leave the house was now a monumental task. It required at least two people, and we had to bring the wheelchair and make sure she was not too tired to speak and still able to hold up her head. Kylie was there, and we jumped into action. Kylie helped get Mom's hair fixed and even put on a little makeup. She still cared about her appearance, as always. I assembled a bag of essentials just in case: towels, neck pillow, sippy cup with juice, and a few medications. It was a twenty-five-minute drive to the church. That was quite a journey in Mom's new world.

The trip was uneventful, and we got the wheelchair out and eased her in it with no problems. There was a long ramp to the office so that was easy enough. I stopped and let his secretary know we had arrived, and we sat in comfortable chairs by the windows in the church office lobby. Mom stayed in the wheelchair since it was rough getting her in and out: her legs didn't provide much support, so it required a full lift.

The church offices were nice with solid wood paneling and heavy upholstered chairs. It was quiet; the only noises were the tapping of the secretary's computer keyboard and an occasional phone ringing. There were magazines on a coffee table: *Faith*, *Catholic Digest*, *U.S. Catholic*, and some church bulletins. Not exactly light reading. Kylie picked one up and quickly put it back down, making a face.

"Grams, they don't have any of your rag mags here, only holy ones."

"Kylie, you should read these. They may help you with your questionable lifestyle." Mom still liked to tease Kylie.

"Sinning is my hobby, Grams. It's good to stay busy." They were both giggling now, and it was refreshing to see that Mom still had full use of her slightly crooked middle finger.

"OK, you guys, can you try to be a little reverent? I know it's hard." I hated having to be the grownup.

"Yeah, Grandma, you totally overuse the finger anyway," Kylie added quietly.

"I have to agree with Kylie on this one. You flip the bird way too much; it hardly has any meaning anymore."

When the words came out of my mouth, she did it again and gave a slight smile. We heard loud footsteps down the hall, and Mom folded her hands in her lap like a mischievous teenager.

"Ah, Suzanne, so nice to see you," Father Rich said as he bent down to give her a hug. "Is that Julie, too? I haven't seen you in so long. How are you?"

"Hi, Father, yes, it's been since I moved across town five years ago." I was trying to imply that I still went to church on the other side of town, which was a lie. I hadn't been to church with any regularity since I moved. I felt guilty, but sometimes life gets in the way. I needed to reexamine my priorities, which was one of the lessons this experience had taught me. Mom's faith was increasingly tenacious, and she used that strength to get her through the worst days.

"And who is this?" Father put his hand out to Kylie, who stood and shook it.

"Hi, Father, I'm the granddaughter, Kylie. I'm visiting from Denver."

"Oh my, I can see the resemblance among all of you. What a blessing to have such a beautiful family, Suzanne. It is so nice to have you all here. I have set aside a good amount of time to meet with you. Do you want to head into my office?"

She nodded. I know she was trying to conserve her speech so that she could talk to him in the closed session. I wheeled her into the office and got her settled.

"Do you need a drink?" I asked, positioning her across from his desk.

She nodded since it helped her speak a little more clearly. I put a sippy cup with apple juice on the table next to her, and I could tell she wanted to be alone with Father, so I left.

He called Kylie and me into the office about forty-five minutes later, and we held hands with Mom and prayed for serenity and peace for all of us. He hugged Mom, held her hands and gave her a kiss on the cheek. She thanked him for the visit as tiny tears sneaked out of the corners of her eyes.

Father then explained to me quietly as Kylie was wheeling Mom out into the hall that I could call him for last rites, and that he would do everything he could to make it over in time. "She's a remarkably strong woman," he said. He then told me how to reach him in an emergency and gave me a quick hug.

On the drive home, we talked about everything except her meeting. Ky and I had become experts at creating light banter to keep everyone's mind off the inevitable. We talked about the traffic, pop culture, reality shows—anything really, as long as it was light and breezy. It was important to keep Mom calm to avoid a flare up. If she didn't offer information, it was not our business to ask.

She was starting to get her things in order, and as close as we all were, we knew it was a very private issue for her.

It was late afternoon now, and Mom was exhausted. I had to put the neck pillow on her when we got into the car because her chin was down to her chest and she couldn't hold her head up. At home, she immediately went to bed without speaking since she had no energy. Winnie went into the room while I got Mom settled but then left with me. For some reason, Winnie wasn't sleeping in there much anymore, even though I tried to get her to stay. She slept in our room, so I finally gave in and moved her dog bed. I read once that dogs can detect serious diseases in their owners through their sense of smell. Winnie seemed to sense that something was wrong and was often visibly affected. Mom must have noticed, but she didn't say anything. Winnie still sat by her in the family room and craved her attention, but the codependency had dropped significantly.

I came back into the kitchen, where Kylie was sitting on a stool at the island. "She's really getting weak, Mom." There were tears in her eyes.

"I know, sweetie. I can see little differences every day. I think I need to have a meeting with the hospice team and see what's going on. I feel like they aren't here enough lately to really evaluate the changes and guide us on what to expect."

"Mom, you need to do that. I'd like to go, but I can stay with Grandma if you want Mark to go with you."

I already had my phone in my hands and left a voicemail with Molly about going to lunch. I also suggested inviting Michelle, our caseworker from hospice. Michelle had been over a few times and called to check in about every two weeks. She provided resources, like a volunteer who helped with showers every three days since my mom didn't want me to shower her anymore. Michelle also had a psychologist make a house call a few months before, but that poor guy hadn't been back. Even though he was attractive and sensitive, Mom wasn't interested in much of anything he had to say about how to cope.

I guess it was something she had to do on her own.

Chapter 28
The Visitors

OLIVER'S WEDDING WAS A FEW WEEKS AWAY, and I was very apprehensive about heading out of town. I wanted to support him and be there for the big day, but I wasn't sure I could. Hopefully, the hospice meeting with Molly and Michelle would give me some clarity. Many things were changing, and I didn't know what to expect next.

The mornings were becoming much more challenging. Mom woke up early to go to the bathroom with help but then immediately went back to bed. She didn't wake again until closer to 11:30 or noon some days. Once she was out of bed and sitting at the table for her breakfast shake, she'd break down. It was a common occurrence. I'm sure the thought of what was happening to her had been pushed into the background when she was medicated and sleeping. But once her thoughts became clear in the morning, it hit her like a ton of bricks. Sad revelations came roaring to the front of her brain and consumed her waking thoughts.

It was heartbreaking to see it play out each morning on a continual loop with little variation. She didn't talk, just cried, and shook as her tears fell onto the placemat in front of her. My reaction had become routine. I would put down whatever I was doing, quietly walk over, and rub her back and hug her through it. My goal was always to get her to breathe slowly before it became a full-blown incident. When she was in distress, it seemed the brain struggled more to get signals to her lung muscles, and her breathing became even weaker. I was, of course, always crying myself, just hiding it from her as best I could.

When Kylie was there, she took it on, and Mark did as well. It was emotional and so draining, but we pressed ahead and always tried to lighten the mood as soon as we felt it was subsiding. That morning, I tried to redirect the energy.

"Hey, Mom, this is some good news. I got a call from Jen late last night, and she wants to visit this weekend. What do you think?"

"She does? That would be nice. Is she bringing the kids?" Mom was wiping her eyes with a napkin.

"Yes, she said she wanted to bring all of them. Do you feel up to that? Maybe just Saturday and then stay over one night? It could be really fun."

My sister has four kids ranging in age from six to twenty-two. She had the two older ones and then years later had two more. The oldest was in college so it was nice he would visit. We were all becoming more aware that each event may be the last.

"I do want to see them, yes. They should come." Her words were slow and almost unrecognizable. It sounded like her tongue was three times its normal size. It improved as the day went on, but her speech was never totally clear anymore.

"Great, I'll let her know and make a plan. What sounds good for a family dinner on Saturday night?"

"Nothing, so you guys just pick something." Mom wasn't eating anymore unless I forced the issue.

"Grams, maybe you and I could make a fun dessert. I'm sure we could avoid poisoning the family if we really focused," Kylie said, and they giggled.

We decided to have a makeshift picnic that day, just sitting on the deck. Mom requested that we get outside and enjoy the sunshine. We brought out some snacks, knowing full well that she wouldn't eat them, along with an Ensure mixed with chocolate syrup in a sippy cup. Winnie came with us and proceeded to explore the woods and crash through the bushes.

"Grams, have you spoken to Kent lately?" Kylie asked.

"Oh yes, I talked to him a few days ago, but it wasn't a very long conversation." She paused and took a drink. Conversation was a huge effort for her, but we still wanted to talk like we always did. "He wants to come over, but I told him no. I'm not up to that visit anymore. It's hard to be alluring when I can't get my balance. Believe me, I've tried." We all laughed.

"I don't think he's expecting sexy, Mom."

"Yes, but I am," she said. "I can't just let it all go."

I understood what she meant and tried to keep it moving. "He's such a great guy. Everybody loves Kent. Oliver told me he's really helping out with Friendly Neighbors and has all sorts of amazing business contacts."

"Yup, we all love Kent, Grandma. Nice catch, hottie," Kylie said.

"It's tough to find the really good ones. Did I ever tell you guys the day that I thought Mark might be the sweetest man ever created?" I asked them.

"No, Mom, but do tell." Kylie shifted in her chair and got comfortable.

"So, we were on a trip in Grand Cayman and had been out on two scuba dives that morning. On our second dive of the day, the sun shone down into the warm water and the fish were purple and yellow and so curious that they swam right up to us. We saw sea turtles floating by and lobsters sitting on the bottom between rocks and all kinds of big fish, too, even a nurse shark. It was awe-inspiring and we got lost in that kind of beauty. As we were making our ascent up the line, I realized that I had to pee.

"Normally, you would just pee in the ocean, but they tell you not to pee in the wetsuits because the charter boat rents them to you. I tried not to think about my bladder, but I was surrounded by water and I couldn't help it, so I eventually gave in. I figured that by the time I got to the surface, it would have rinsed out. You have to stop for decompression breaks and so it takes a while to get to the top. When I reached the back of the boat, Mark was there at the same time and the dive instructors helped us both out of the water.

"Just then, one of the instructors said, 'Somebody peed in the wetsuit. I smell pee. Yup, one of you peed!'

"I was stunned and froze. And just when I was about to sheepishly admit to it, Mark said, 'Yup, sorry guys it was me. Couldn't wait. I'll scrub it out.'

"They proceeded to lecture him on it, and I scurried off. Later, I whispered, 'Wow, you took the hit for me, you are so sweet.'

"He stopped and said, 'Oh wow, did you pee in your suit, too?'"

Mom and Kylie laughed as I delivered the punchline.

"So, you thought he was the sweetest but learned it was all about him," Mom slowly managed to get out.

"Yes, that pretty much sums it up, Mom."

We had fun sharing funny stories about men for another hour until she began dozing off in the sunshine. We took her inside for a nap.

My sister and her four children arrived that Saturday morning and were surprised that Mom was still sleeping. They had not seen her for a few weeks, so I knew there would be a shock. I felt compelled to prepare them.

"Jen, I know you've had chats with her on the phone, but I just want to tell you guys that she has lost more weight and is getting very tired much easier these days." This explanation was for the kids since I knew they might not be able to disguise their shock. "She will probably get up in about an hour and I know she'll be so happy to see you guys. She uses the wheelchair all the time now, so you can help her with that. Also, she'll want to watch a movie with you, so maybe start thinking about some ideas."

The movie was something we had talked about the previous day, and Mom felt it could help her not to have to talk too much but still be with the kids. Talking was becoming exceedingly difficult, and her jaw had started to slip out of place occasionally. If we massaged her cheek, we could usually get it back in place. These were small but very recognizable signs that the muscles were deteriorating in all sorts of strange ways. Some days she couldn't lift her cup, the next day she could. One morning, she couldn't hold her head up for more than an hour, the next day, it was easy again. I could never have imagined the sheer horror of the disease and how it seemed to ebb and flow before eventually returning permanently. It was a slow and tortuous process.

"It would be fun to watch *Frozen* again. Grandma likes that movie," Eve added, overly excited.

"We'll let her pick the movie, Eve," Avery said, overruling her much-too-eager little sister.

We organized the little kids in the family room and the older two went into the kitchen to stare at their phones. I pulled Jenny into the living room to talk.

"Hey, Sis, how are you doing these days?" I asked her.

"Fucking shitty, Sis. How are you doing these days?" she said flatly.

"Yes, fucking shitty is a good description. Thanks for asking." I smirked and continued. "I told you about the jaw stuff, didn't I? It's bizarre that it just falls out of the socket on the left side. She says it doesn't hurt, but I don't think it's going to go back in place one of these times. I called Sarah over yesterday, since I thought a dentist would know what to do, and she moved it around and said she has an oral surgeon friend we should see. She thinks he can put a screw in there and keep it attached. I'm not sure if that's something we should do, but it's an option. I just feel like the pace of decline has really picked up lately, and I'm cracking, Jen."

I felt the tears form out of the blue, and she started crying, too. We were clinging together on the living room sofa when I heard a familiar noise on the monitor speaker I kept at my side.

"Can you get me, please?"

Jen and I wiped our faces and walked down the hall and into her darkened room. Mom liked the blinds pulled during the day, and I always opened them when I got her up, so it didn't seem so glum.

Jen went right to her and started helping her up. "Hi, Mom. It's so good to see you. The kids are really excited to hang out with you."

Mom looked right through her like she didn't recognize her. She was disoriented. I walked over and got in front of her face.

"Hi, Mom. Are you still waking up?" I said loudly to get her attention.

"Ohhh, yes, I'm a little out of it. Jenny, I'm happy to see you." She turned her attention to Jen and her voice was cracking and slurred, but we could tell what she said. They embraced for a good long time and then we helped her get into the bathroom.

She was very slow that day, and I hoped the visit would go OK. When we got her out to the kitchen in the wheelchair, the kids were quiet for a minute but acclimated as kids always do. They were very attentive and talked to her all about school and their pets, and the older kids helped with her pillows and blankets, and it was sweet. They watched a movie and even read to her. Overall, it was a good day. She got tired, so we wheeled her to the bedroom for a nap before dinner. As we were getting her settled in bed, she had a severe coughing attack that we couldn't get under control with the usual methods. I resorted to using the liquid morphine, and she was out for hours afterward. She missed dinner, and I finally woke her at 7:30 so she could see the family. She was too tired, and we just did the bedtime routine and medication, so she could sleep for the night.

We convened in the lower level for wine after dinner. Kylie, Jen, Mark, and I bellied up on the barstools and turned on some music. The kids were in the room next door playing video games. I had the monitor sitting on the bar top close to me. We talked about the past few weeks, and how things had been declining, and some of the ridiculous things Mom had said. She really was hilarious and kept us laughing.

"She was reminiscing last week and told me that she had wanted to run a bed and breakfast as her retirement plan," I said. "She described an old farmhouse near the lake in Grand Haven with a long porch and gorgeous gardens for her guests. Her thought was that it would be a great way to meet people but then realized she didn't want to clean the bedrooms or cook breakfast. That kind of ruined the whole concept of a bed and breakfast. She is such a nut."

It got quiet as we all realized how much we were going to miss that crazy lady. Anytime I slowed down—whenever I stopped moving, really—hopelessness and despair hit me like a Mack truck. The pain was almost debilitating, so I forced myself to press on.

"I hate to bring this up, Julie, but has she said anything about what she wants for a funeral? I know we need to talk about it at some point, as much as I hate to," Jen said.

"She told me she wants an elaborate affair and actually plans to show up as a spirit to see who is distraught and crying and who are the assholes that never really loved her," Kylie said, as we laughed.

"Oh, yeah, she told me something like that, too, and if there's anyone she thinks is not sufficiently bereaved, she will torture them from beyond. She's really counting on having some afterlife powers," I added, and we giggled. It felt good to laugh.

"But she has mentioned a few things that she wants. She made it clear she does not want an open casket. She wants to be cremated." I paused, knowing this would be a hard sell for my sister.

Jen's expression changed. She was the strictest Catholic in our family and didn't like that idea. Just then, I heard a voice on the monitor. It was low, and I couldn't make out the words, but it was Mom. Kylie grabbed the monitor and put it up to her ear.

"She sounds like she's talking to someone. Are any of the kids upstairs?" Kylie asked Jen.

Jenny got off her barstool and poked her head in the next room. "No, they're all in there."

Kylie still had the monitor speaker to her ear.

"What is she saying, Kylie? Does she need someone?" Mark asked.

"Not really, but she's having a conversation of some kind. There are breaks and then she talks again. It's weird. I'm going to go check on her." Kylie took off up the stairs.

"It sounds like the time she was convinced she had a conversation with Aunt Kink," I said to Jen.

"Oh my God, this is kind of creepy, Julie. Do you really think she's seeing people?" Jen gasped.

"Yeah, I do, and Mark has agreed. This has happened a few times."

"Yup." Mark looked at Jen and nodded. "She's having conversations with people who have died."

We all sat focused on the monitor as the conversation continued.

"I've been trying to get organized, but I am so tired. I know it's getting close."

"Yes, I'll do that soon. I know that I need to, Mom."

"OK, I'm going to rest now. I'm very tired."

Chapter 29
The Lunch

AFTER JEN AND THE KIDS departed on Sunday, I immediately resumed my caretaking routine.

"Hey, Mom, do you remember having a conversation with your mom? It was the night that Jenny and the kids were here. Kylie came up and talked to you in your room, and you said you were talking to her," I said casually as I loaded the dishwasher.

"Of course, I do, Julie. You don't think that you would forget a conversation with Vicki, do you? I haven't seen her in fifteen years, and even though we were never close, it was kind of a big deal to talk to her again. Of course, I remember," she said slowly.

"Umm, OK, Mom. It just sounds a little weird, that's all."

"It's not weird at all. She's just concerned about me and wanted to talk about getting things organized. She's been through this already, you know. She really wanted me to tell you what I wanted for a funeral and where all the papers and insurance information are stored. She was kind of bossy, now that I think about it," she said and laughed.

"Was it good to see her?"

"Yes, but it seemed like she was in a bad mood."

"Oh my God, this is strange, Mom. Have you seen a lot of people?" I decided to go all in on that topic.

"There've been a few old friends who have passed, including my sister and now my mother." She paused for a few seconds. "But the person I would really like to talk to is my dad, and for some reason, he hasn't visited at all."

We sat in silence for a few minutes, and I could feel her sadness about the lost past and her fading future. I wasn't sure what to make of these ethereal conversations, but they seemed to make her feel better, and who knows what the afterlife holds? I was just happy that she seemed to be at peace with the inevitable. She was handling it better than I was. I tried to focus on the positive.

"I'm sure that will be an incredible reunion, Mom. It will be great to see him, you just aren't ready yet. He's going to have to wait!"

"Yes, I'm looking forward to seeing him, just not quite yet." I gave her a side hug, and we talked about the day ahead.

Kylie was heading over to spend the day. She was coming to the house much more often now that my mom's care level had increased. Mom was sleeping more and getting her to eat was a real chore. I was always bargaining and negotiating. There was a sense of accomplishment if she got a full calorie bomb shake down in the morning. I had to constantly coax her to take a drink and then another one. This badgering went on for hours, and most days, that was the majority of what she consumed since she couldn't swallow solid food.

Kylie came through the door and immediately sat at the table by her grandma. After the hugging stopped, Kylie wasted no time in getting to questions.

"So, Grams, I want to hear all about the conversation with my great-grandma. What the hell were you gabbing about?"

Mom swallowed hard to pool her limited resources to talk. "I just told your mom that she was really kind of bitchy and just kept bugging me about getting my papers organized."

Kylie roared. "Well, isn't that rude, to visit someone from beyond and act snippy! How dare she give you tasks to complete! I barely remember her, but didn't she make those awful cookies? Who thinks that cookies should have figs and dates in them? That is *not* what a cookie is supposed to be. And then the nuts, too. She really ruined cookies for us," Kylie snarked.

"I always thought she was pretty sharp, quite a snappy dresser," I added.

"She was an interesting woman. Not warm in the traditional sense, and I don't ever remember her hugging me as a child. She always had so many stressors in her life after Dad died. And she never, ever said, 'I love you,'" Mom said slowly as she looked out the window.

We wandered off onto other topics and had a nice day even though Mom was fatigued. I kept thinking it was from all the activity from the weekend. She napped most of the day and joined us for a light dinner. I got her ready for bed on the usual schedule, paying close attention to the drugs and the timeline.

When she was fully snuggled into bed, she grabbed my arm and said, "Don't go just yet. I want to talk to you."

I pulled one of the upholstered chairs to the side of her bed and waited for her to begin.

"Julie, I need you to know that I feel like this is starting to take me over. I'm getting weaker and I don't have too much fight left in me. Even though my mom seemed bitchy, she's right, and I should tell you what I'm thinking about a funeral." She took a long pause and gathered her thoughts and her strength. I instantly reached for her hand, knowing this was a tough topic. "I can't have people looking at my dead body and the withered person I've become. You must promise to cremate me. I know your sister doesn't like the idea, but please promise me."

"I promise, Mom."

"Julie, also, I don't want any weird visitation. People hate the awkwardness, and I just don't want to make them do it. Can you just keep it to a funeral at the church and some beautiful songs and, of course, flowers? That's all I want, OK?"

"OK, Mom, of course. But what about a luncheon at the Sculpture Gardens? That would be beautiful. I really want to do that and have everyone outside having lunch surrounded by all those beautiful gardens. It would be simply perfect. Is that acceptable?"

"Hell no, Julie. I don't want you guys spending money on an expensive lunch. Maybe you could do something at the church. I've volunteered there for years. I'm sure they want to have a luncheon for me."

"That's not what I envisioned. You are too special for that. We will see." I squeezed her hand lightly, indicating that there was not much she could do about it. She seemed pleased to have gotten that off her chest, and she drifted off to sleep.

The next day was the lunch scheduled with Molly the hospice nurse and Michelle, the hospice social worker. Mark and I were going to meet them at Applebee's at noon. We got there first and chose a booth along the windows.

"So, do you have a plan for this conversation?" Mark said as he picked up one of the brightly colored menus.

"Not really. But as you and I have talked about, I feel like she has really declined lately, and I want to see what they think."

"It seems like we're not all on the same page, and I think it's because they don't see her enough. It's almost like when Molly is there, Mom tries so hard to seem more alert."

"They usually visit her in mid-afternoon, which is after her nap, and she's doing pretty well. Which is fine, I just think I have a better picture than they do."

"You definitely do, Julie. Let's see what they think since I know you are anxious about leaving in a few weeks to go to Oliver's wedding."

"Yeah, I hope they have some insight. Given how I feel right now, I can't really see going."

Mark and I had discussed it, and I didn't have any idea how I could leave for three full days. I really wanted to be there for Oliver's big day, but the timing was working against us.

Molly and Michelle came in together. Over the years, they had been assigned to many cases as a team, and I could see that they seemed to value each other's opinions when I had been able to talk to them together (which was rare).

"Thanks so much for meeting us. I never get to talk to both of you together, and this seemed like a good way to catch up away from our house," I said, offering them a selection from the appetizer sampler.

"It is really nice. Rarely do clients invite us to lunch. In fact, this might be the first time," Michelle said, and Molly laughed and nodded.

Mark took a stab at laying the groundwork. "Well, we're really glad that you could make the time. Julie and I are concerned that Suzanne has been declining rather rapidly lately. In fact, her jaw slipping out of place has become a real problem and is further delaying eating, and even talking. Also, she is sleeping a lot more during the day. And as you both know she is still losing weight. We've never been able to get that stabilized."

As he spoke, I felt my eyes starting to moisten and sting. I was hearing it from a third party, and it resonated loud and clear. It was all true, and the totality of it made me genuinely concerned. Thinking about it altogether, I was sure that we were nearing a new, final phase. When Mark finished talking, he looked over at me. I didn't want to add anything since I thought I might start crying and ruin lunch.

Michelle, our caseworker, also looked at me and responded quickly, "Julie, I know you guys are really concerned. I can see it, but I have been doing this for more than twenty years. Your mom is doing fairly well and may have a good amount of time left."

Molly agreed. "We were discussing this on the phone before we got here. I have been nursing hospice patients, and particularly ALS patients, for more than twelve years, and if we had to put a number on it—which we don't like to do—your mom has about four to six months."

I gasped. "Four to six months? Are you sure? She's really starting to suffer, and I don't know how she can stand it that long. Why do you think that?" I was tearing up now.

Molly reached for my hand. "Listen. Her vitals are actually fine. She has a good pulse and heart rate. Her breathing level seems to have diminished, but she is doing surprisingly well. I know you guys see her the most but in total, and with the data we have, she is doing fine."

I sat there in complete silence. The last thing that I had always held out hope for was that there would be no suffering. This fucked-up disease would take what it came for but let's not drag her through a horrible, tortuous process. I prayed that she could pass peacefully, surrounded by loved ones, when the time came. I couldn't stand to see her suffering and deteriorating as her agony was prolonged!

"So, am I supposed to get to a point where I'm just administering morphine to keep her unconscious? Her last days spent in a completely drugged and lethargic state? It's horrific to see her gasping for air in an all-out panic!"

Mark put his hand on top of mine to calm me down. "I think Julie just wants to know what to expect next. Honestly, we haven't been given much direction from you guys, and we're at the point where we obviously need some," Mark added softly. He was playing the role of good cop.

"Of course, we need to try to guide you, but every case is different, and hopefully your mom's case will be without trauma. That's why we have Dr. Phillips engaged at regular intervals so he can monitor the situation. We want to help you through this as best we can," Michelle said.

I think they were a little scared of my current emotional state. I could see the questioning glances between them when the waitress came back to deliver our salad and sandwich orders.

"Do you think you need us to schedule more visits? Would that help?" Molly asked when the waitress was out of earshot.

"Yes, I think that would help. I just feel like there is more going on than you get to see, and I'm very concerned. As Mark said, she's sleeping more, she hallucinates sometimes, she's often confused, and the breathing incidents are daily now," I said, trying to be pragmatic and less emotional.

"My main concern is that she will contract pneumonia or suffer heart failure, but there are no signs of either of those conditions." Molly was talking between bites of a club sandwich. "Let's move our visits up to four days a week, and we can schedule Dr. Phillips to come over next week and see what he thinks as well."

"Yes, I think that makes sense. I'll make a new schedule for Suzanne when I get back to the office, and we can put that in motion starting next week," Michelle said as she poured all the dressing from the ramekin onto her healthy salad.

"Well, my main concern at this very minute is the wedding of my business partner in Traverse City in two weeks. I just don't feel like I should leave her."

"Julie, caregivers need support, too. Caregiving is physically and emotionally exhausting. Over time, you can burn out, or worse, get sick yourself. It would do you good to take some time to recharge. I think it's a good idea to go to that wedding and try to enjoy yourself. You have no idea the huge toll this is taking on you. Actually, both of you," Michelle said, directing that last sentence to Mark. He didn't take the bait, and we continued to pick at our lunch.

This exchange reminded me of one of the pamphlets Molly had left on the kitchen island for me, *Help Guide for a Caregiver*. It warned of the signs and symptoms of caregiver stress. I checked off eight of the ten boxes listed. After reading it for a few minutes, I threw it into the wastebasket. I then proceeded to pour a large glass of wine in direct disregard of the number one "don't" on the list of ways to manage burnout. *Avoid drinking too much alcohol*. What do they know?

After some other discussion, we finished up our lunch and recapped the newly proposed schedule. They complimented us on the great care that we had been giving Mom and said that was most likely why she was doing so well. I was tuned out because I was still wondering how she would be able to go on for another four to six months! It just didn't seem possible since even with all my pleading and pushing of food, she was probably under 100 pounds. I didn't know how to get her to eat more, and she was well past the feeding tube stage, something she refused on several occasions. Watching helplessly as someone starves to death was unimaginable. I wasn't sure how much longer I could hold on.

Chapter 30
The Shells

WE DROVE AROUND for a few minutes until I could pull it together, and then headed back to the house. It seemed like Kylie and Mom had enjoyed a nice afternoon. Mom thought that we were out shopping for furniture because we didn't want to tell her where we were going. I hated to keep secrets from her, but I also didn't want to alarm her. Overall, her attitude was surprisingly good most of the time except for the moments in the morning when she woke up depressed.

After Mom settled into a nap, Kylie eased onto the kitchen island stool and faced me. "She didn't have a very alert day today, Mom. She seemed a little disoriented and asked me a few times where you were, not remembering the answer from a few minutes earlier. She was confused about Winnie, too, and wanted me to let her outside every five minutes, and then asked where she was. What did you find out today?"

"It's good news, although I'm not sure how to assess it at this moment. They think she has four to six months and feel she's doing well."

"Wow, that's great. I am glad to hear it ... aren't you?"

"Yes, of course, but I just don't know how bad it will get, and I'm worried that it will be unbearable for her. She's been declining rather quickly lately, and I just don't want her to suffer. That's been my concern since we knew this was terminal." I started to cry, and she did, too. We shuddered together for a moment and then let go. Our ability to cry in any position—hug, non-hug, sitting, standing—was a skill we had mastered out of necessity.

"They're going to be here more, and the doctor is going to make another visit so that I can feel confident to go to the wedding."

"Mom, I can help out more, too. Staying at Dad's across town is taking too much travel time now. I felt it was good to have one less body here, but the situation has changed. How about I move in over the weekend? And maybe we should have a few other people here while you're gone. I'm sure Aunt Jen would come, and maybe even your brothers. I can reach out to them if you want."

"Kylie, that would help. Thanks, sweetie."

We stopped crying and grabbed some paper towels from the counter. We never wanted to be too far from our paper product these days.

Mom slept for a long time, and I went into the room to check on her. I said her name softly and touched her hand. Her eyelids fluttered open, and I whispered, "Mom, are you ready to get up and have something to drink, or maybe watch a show, or we could read together?"

She didn't respond right away, just looked at me for a few seconds. Slowly, she muttered through her constantly dry lips, "Just want to sleep longer."

"You've been in here for at least three hours. Don't you want to get up before dinner?"

She shook her head very slowly and sank back to sleep. I left but came back about twenty minutes later and tried again. This time, she was more alert.

"Julie, what time is it?"

"It's about 5:00 in the afternoon, Mom. I'd like to get you up for a little while, and Mark is putting together a nice dinner for us tonight. Kylie is here, too."

"OK, I'll get up." I could tell her jaw had slipped out of place again, and I could barely decipher what she was saying. I proceeded to massage the left side of her face, but it didn't help this time. Having no viable options, I reluctantly left it alone. Getting her out of bed was now a three-step process. First, I pulled the wheelchair over to the side of the bed. Then I raised her hospital bed up to get her into a sitting position. Finally, I gently pulled her legs over to the side of the bed and helped lift her into the chair. She didn't weigh much, so it was easy. An occupational therapist had visited a few weeks earlier to show me the proper way to help her do many things without hurting either of us.

Mom settled into the family room sofa with Winnie sitting by her legs and Kylie next to her. I went to help Mark.

"Is she OK, Julie? She seems disoriented."

"Yes, I noticed that. It comes and goes, but I think if I had left her alone today, she would have just kept on sleeping. She doesn't have any energy and needs the BiPAP more frequently now to breathe. Also, her jaw is out of place on the left again. I'm hoping to get her to drink a calorie bomb tonight."

"That would be good. Hopefully, she can get some of it down," Mark said quietly. We both knew that would be more than she had consumed in the past few days.

As predicted, she didn't really drink much, and it sat in front of her during dinner. She had a faraway look most of the time. Kylie kept asking her questions that were met with long, distant stares before she nodded or shook her head slowly. Kylie looked distressed and just kept talking.

"Hey, Grams, do you remember when I was about six years old and we were on vacation in Naples, Florida? I was so confused that the beach didn't have all the pretty shells like Sanibel Island does. It had so much sand, and I kept asking you where all the shells were because I knew sometimes shells make sand. You told me that can be true when the shells get crushed up into tiny pieces, and that all we needed to do was just keep looking for a big one. And then one day when we went down to the beach and I was searching for any kind of shell, I found a huge one that just happened to wash up. Do you remember that Grandma?"

My mom was looking at her and smiled slightly. She nodded her head, but her chin was down to her chest, so Kylie didn't see it. I got up to find her neck pillow and put it on her. Kylie continued with the story.

"That's because you snuck to the gift shop on the corner and bought it and then slyly dropped it right in front of me, so I would find it washing up in the surf! I was so excited to have found that big conch shell. I didn't realize you planted it until just a few years ago. It was so awesome, Grams. It made me so happy. I took it to school and told everyone that I'd found it on the beach. You have always been the best grandmother to me." Kylie had a small, sparkling tear on her cheek, and she seemed desperate for a reaction.

Mom smiled again after struggling to get an expression but didn't say anything. After she dozed off a few times at the table, I asked her if she wanted to get ready for bed. She slowly nodded. We quietly went through the process of getting her nighttime drugs and I got her settled in. I pulled the chair up to the side of her bed and took her hand.

"You doing OK, Mom? What can I do for you tonight?"

She whispered softly and slowly so I bent in close to understand, "Tell me about the shells on the beach, Julie."

"We're walking down the beach on a sunny, breezy afternoon. Our bare feet are trying to avoid all the small, scattered shells with the sharp edges, but we step on one every now and then that hurts a little. We are looking down as we walk because you never know what treasure you might find half-buried in the sand or rolling up with the surf. The pelicans are flying a few inches off the water looking for an early dinner, their throats noticeably swallowing as they scoop up fish. Those cute yellow-footed birds you love are gathered in groups running frantically in and out of the waves catching minnows. We notice a dolphin surface between the whitecaps, and we stop to see if it will come up again. There are low-roaring boat motors and children chattering while playing in the background behind us. The soft breeze and the rhythm of the surf have us in a beautiful beach trance. There is an elaborate shell-encrusted sandcastle up ahead, and we walk toward it as we hold hands and think about how lucky we are to be in such a beautiful place together."

As I said this, I gave her hand a soft squeeze and noticed that she was peacefully asleep and probably had been for the past few seconds, so I quit talking. I adjusted her blankets, turning them down just under her chin. Then I kissed her forehead and let go of her hand. I partially closed her blinds, so the direct sun wouldn't wake her in the morning, and softly pulled the door.

I woke the next morning to the sound of the clock's second hand clicking away as Mark snored softly and Winnie lay motion-less. This was truly a luxury. I wasn't used to sleeping in, and it felt good. Mom must have been overly tired from last night's activities, but I couldn't let her sleep too long. I put on my slippers and walked to her door. Opening it a crack, I could see the sun shining on her face through the blinds. Despite her peaceful appearance, I screamed and ran to her, but there was nothing to do. I held her and wept hysterically. I eventually caught my breath and looked up to see Mark at my side.

He held me for a long time, rubbing my back and head, and whispering repeatedly, "She knew."

Epilogue

THIS BOX IS AN UNMANAGEABLE SIZE, and I am trying to slide it into the living room to start the packing, but I can't get a grip on it. It is tall and awkward; meant to hold a few pieces of large wall art and I am feeling uncoordinated. We have hired a moving crew and they will be here tomorrow to do much of the organizing, but I have a few of our treasured items that I am supposed to be protecting and packing. My pace has been slow, and I don't care if I get all my "assignments" done today, since I feel spent. I have just finished clearing out her bedroom where the last remnants of clothes, plants, books, and cards had been left.

I got lost in the sorting and examined each item as if I was seeing it for the first time. It's my own fault that there are still things in that room. I could not bring myself to sweep the last memories away, but now I have no choice. We are leaving and the thought that this will be our last night in this house is bittersweet. I will miss living here but learned very quickly that every quiet hallway and serene window view holds a memory that makes me want to back up time. Life often seems suspended, and I have been unable to gain momentum, so a change of scenery makes sense. Mark's business is taking off in Detroit, which is good timing.

I pull the framed picture over the living room fireplace mantle off its hooks and ease it to the ground. It's the first one that I surround with packing paper and stuff into the box. Looking at the empty mantle, I remember the last Christmas in this room when my family gathered after Mom died and the struggle that we all went through to just get through the day. The mood was uncomfortably somber, not our normal energized holiday. I had barely made much of an effort, even Christmas had lost some of its shine. Holidays remind us of the deep emptiness that losing a loved one conjures. That emptiness may fade, but it will always be there just waiting to spring sadness with a memory or a conversation.

Mark and I have purchased an older home on Lake St. Clair. It has amazing views of the water and room for a boat dock. It's older and in rough shape, so it will need to be remodeled and I welcome the distraction.

Kylie reluctantly went back to Denver after many discussions about staying. She was very worried and wanted to keep an eye on me, but eventually had to get back to her life and it was the best thing to do.

Lately, I have heard the sweet optimism creep back into her voice and it makes me happy that she is finding her own way to move on. We talk on the phone almost daily but try to keep the topics to bright subjects and positive news. Yesterday, she notified me that she has arranged a job transfer back to this area and is even looking at homes.

I had an opportunity to sell my company about six months ago and jumped at the chance. It has expanded into other areas like mobile marketing and niche products. I had buried myself in work to avoid the grief, and when I finally came up for air, it all seemed like a silly venture. I had started to check out mentally, so the sale gave me the option to see the company grow from afar with no direct responsibility.

Winnie is rarely ever more than a few feet away from me, and today she provides a needed distraction. "Oh Winnie, you look like you need to go outside. Do you want to take a walk? I really should be more focused on packing, but it's a beautiful day. Let's do it!"

She immediately jumps up and down since she knows what "outside" and "walk" mean. I grab the leash from the mudroom hook and attempt to attach it to her collar.

"OK, calm down, spaz. We can go but you need to stand still for just one second."

She finally stops jumping, we get organized and head out the side door.

"You're going to have to become a lake dog instead of a woods dog soon, Winnie. That means trading the war with squirrels for a battle with ducks and geese. How do you feel about that? I know you are an excellent swimmer so I think you will like the new digs."

She wags her tail at the mention of her name and starts sniffing for creatures. I have a lot of discussions with Winnie these days. She's not much of a conversationalist but an excellent listener. We both miss my mom terribly and we share those thoughts and memories when we are home alone most days.

The air is crisp and feels like fall is dancing on the edges. The woods are starting to change colors and the sun is breaking through the umbrella of branches. These surroundings always give me a chance to reflect on things that are still rolling around in my head. For the longest time, I tried to call my mom on the phone just about every other day. I had random thoughts about things I needed to tell her. I also planned holidays and events with her in mind only to realize that she wouldn't be there. But the one thing that consumes my thoughts is the last night, simply because I feel cheated. It was an unfair ending that I did not expect. I had so many things that I wanted to say to her, so many moments to laugh and hold each other. I had her to myself for months and there were still things I wanted to say. I ask myself, how I could be so stupid and not know that was her last night?

Many well-meaning people have told me that she left so abruptly on purpose and didn't want to drag out her disease. That she wanted to spare us, and especially me, all the horrible suffering. I think that's bullshit. I have had a lot of time to think and I have my own theory and it is the one that comforts me.

Since she had already told me on numerous occasions that she was having afterlife visitors, I think that my grandfather, her father, made a visit to her room that night. He asked her to come with him and she was ready, so she did. It was what she had been waiting for, her body was tired, and it was all that she needed to let go. It was peaceful, and she was serene and happy.

This version helps me relax and understand the beautiful symmetry of our lives. It gives me a sense of calm in the debilitating loss of her. It also provides some clarity to the confusing trajectory of a terminal illness. She fought so valiantly and focused on grace and even laughter in the constant shadow of the inevitable. Even in the end, she was protecting us as she always had.

My mom's struggle reminded me that life isn't about work or money or status. It's about caring for each other through the good times and the bad. Ultimately, it's about family, even if that includes an unruly but loveable Labradoodle.

Acknowledgements

FOR YOUR early and generous support, and helpful comments, I want to thank Elaine Cullen, Amy Foster Kuzdowicz, Shelly Anderson and Laura Light. You are my trusted readers and helped me so much to keep going in this process.

I would also like to acknowledge my friend and editor, Dave Smitherman, who showed me the way to bring greater depth and shape to my personal story. Also, my agent, Diane Nine, who believed in the power and marketability of this project. Your guidance was immeasurable.

I am extremely grateful to my family; my generous and supportive dad, amazing brothers Jeffrey and Jonathon, and my wonderful sister Jenny, who has held my hand on numerous occasions.

An incredibly special thanks to my husband Mark, who was the first to read a few chapters and encouraged me to keep going. He is also the rock that supported me through the hardest days in 2015 (and every day since). I am so lucky to be your wife.

My amazing daughter Kylie, you are the best of me, and I love your heart and humor and am so grateful to have you in my life. Thank you for all the encouragement, hugs, and support through the years.

Winnie, sweet girl, your unconditional love was the best. Your soulful eyes said everything. I know you and mom are together again eating donuts for dinner.

I would be remiss if I did not acknowledge the thousands of people who are suffering with Amyotrophic Lateral Sclerosis (ALS). This is the most tragic disease, and they deserve to be known and recognized for their perseverance and grace. It's well past time for treatments and a cure.

CPSIA information can be obtained
at www.ICGtesting.com
Printed in the USA
BVHW062017101121
621198BV00008B/853